English madness

English madness

Ideas on insanity, 1580–1890

Vieda Skultans
Lecturer in Mental Health
University of Bristol

Routledge & Kegan Paul
London, Boston and Henley

First published in 1979
by Routledge & Kegan Paul Ltd
39 Store Street, London WC1E 7DD,
Broadway House, Newtown Road,
Henley-on-Thames, Oxon RG9 1EN and
9 Park Street, Boston, Mass. 02108, USA
Set in Times Roman and
printed in Great Britain by
Unwin Bros. Ltd.

British Library Cataloguing in Publication Data

Skultans, Vieda

English Madness
1. Mental illness – Great Britain – Public opinion
2. Public opinion – Great Britain – History
I Title
301.15'43'6168900941   RC455.2.P85   79-41020

ISBN 0 7100 0329 3

Contents

Illustrations

vii

Acknowledgments

I should like to take this opportunity of thanking my friends and colleagues who have helped in the preparation of this book by their encouragement and advice. The book was read in a draft form by Dr Miriam David, Mr Michael Hay and Dr Ian Iamnett. Their comments encouraged me to continue when my optimism had flagged. I also want to thank my colleagues in the Department of Mental Health, who have shown great tolerance of and interest in my work over the past few years. The University of Bristol Publications Fund kindly assisted with a grant towards the cost of typing and Mrs Risdale typed several versions of the manuscript with exactitude and patience.

The author and publisher would like to thank the following for permission to reproduce copyright material: Andrew Scull for extracts from *Museums of Madness,* reprinted by permission of A. D. Peters & Co. Ltd, and the Mary Evans Picture Library for illustrations 1-11; illustrations 12-25 are reproduced by courtesy of the Wellcome Trustees.

1
Introduction

This book deals with a number of themes in the history of insanity. It does not set out to provide a complete history of the period under review, rather it is concerned with issues which, although they may be interesting in themselves, serve to illustrate a more general problem, namely, the relationship between diagnostic categories in psychiatry and social categories. Each chapter is devoted to an exploration of this relationship. For example, notions of feminine vulnerability are shown to be related to the social circumstances which govern women's lives. The 'incurables' of nineteenth-century asylums were drawn almost entirely from the destitute poor. The threat of masturbational insanity was most acute for young middle-class men for whom self-control was a vital ingredient of social and material success. Thus this book is in no sense a history of insanity, but a highly selective collection of chapters on the history of the insane.

This approach differs from some earlier histories of psychiatry. For example, Richard Hunter and Ida Macalpine, editors and authors of several important and interesting books on the history of psychiatry, are clearly committed to the medical model in psychiatry. They write:

> There are conflicting opinions about psychiatry and even among psychiatrists there is hardly a body of knowledge on which all agree. The historians of the contemporary scene must work from a viewpoint. Ours is that psychiatry is foremost a branch of medicine and subject to its discipline. We do not accept that mental illness is somehow different from physical illness as terms like neurosis, psychosis and their

subdivisions imply. Patients suffer from mental symptoms which like bodily symptoms are caused by disease. It is the psychiatrist's task to identify its seat and nature by the methods of modern investigative and laboratory medicine (Hunter and Macalpine, 1974, p.12).

Hunter and Macalpine attribute little importance to the social context within which medicine develops. Social conditions are thought to have an incidental effect on medical ideas, certainly not a formative one. Past theories of insanity are assessed in terms of their similarity to or departure from what present day psychiatrists 'know' about insanity. And yet in an earlier book the authors wrote: 'we turned to history on the sound adage that the history of science is the science itself, hoping to get the present in perspective by tracing the problems of the past and how modern views and trends developed' (Hunter and Macalpine, 1963, p. viii). And elaborating on this position they write: 'Rather than a chronicle of feats, facts and discoveries, the history of psychiatry presents a record of perennial problems, recurrent ideas, disputes and treatments' (ibid., pp. viii-ix). However, although this latter view is not altogether inconsistent with an allegiance to the medical model, neither is it in total harmony with it. If all phases of medical development have equal status, in the sense of being different but equally valid attempts to grapple with recurrent problems, then there are no grounds for arguing the superiority of the medical model. However intriguing Hunter and Macalpine may find the history of psychiatry, their adherence to Goethe's maxim – that the history of a science is the science itself – is tenuous, since earlier ideas about and treatments of insanity are assessed in terms of their approximation to the medical model. The subordinate nature of psychiatry *vis-à-vis* society's needs is not recognized.

Another widely quoted history of psychiatry is by two American psychiatrists Alexander and Seleznick (1967). Their approach is quite different from that of Hunter and Macalpine. Their orientation is psychoanalytic and introspective and they attach great importance to insight. They write:

It appears indeed that man has a deep disinclination to understand the disturbances of his behaviour in terms of psychology. He undoubtedly shuns the responsibility which results from such understanding and is ready to blame the spirits, the devil, or even mystical fluids in his body for his abnormal behaviour instead of recognizing that it is the result of his own feelings, strivings and inner conflicts (ibid., p.13).

Earlier treatments of the insane are valued according to the extent to which they promote insight into inner conflicts.

A rather similar outlook is held by John Howells in his review of the history of psychiatry in Britain. Howells assesses earlier periods in terms of embodiment of psychotherapeutic techniques: 'Materialism slowly but surely steered medicine away from psychopathology and left the psychiatrist in isolation, an alienist. In this context, these 300 years (i.e. from 1600 to 1900) deserve to be termed the dark age of psychiatry' (1975, p.169). For historians of a different orientation the move away from organic explanations during the era of moral management might be said to earn it the title of the dark age. In each case the assessment of the past depends upon current psychiatric orientation.

Another historian of psychiatry whose approach differs markedly from mine is Kathleen Jones. Students and researchers in this area will remain much indebted to her for providing a clear and readily available record of events which would otherwise have remained far less accessible. However as the titles of her books suggest she is interested primarily in the law with regard to lunacy. Her approach, like that of many psychiatrists who embark upon a history of psychiatry, is constrained by the framework of the medical model. Science and, in this instance, psychiatry, are construed as being outside the domain of sociological analysis. Ideas about insanity are judged in terms of their greater or lesser approximation to the position of a kindly and humane psychiatrist of today.

In contrast to these 'straight' historians of psychiatry, Thomas Szasz uses the history of psychiatry to illustrate his views on the nature of psychiatry. According to Szasz institutional psychiatry has one overarching function which is to control behaviour. By a process of semantic conversion, moral terms are translated into medical terms, thereby making them more powerful and effective in regulating behaviour. Medicine, and particularly psychiatry, are the means whereby the dominant values of society are disseminated. By and large psychiatry focuses its spotlight on certain disreputable and marginal elements in society, thus discrediting them and rendering them even weaker. Szasz has found some striking examples to support his view of psychiatry. For example, the famous asylums founded in France during the eighteenth century have some very interesting rules governing admission. Among the categories of persons to be admitted are the young who disobey their parents and refuse to work and unmarried women with child. Although it is recognized that asylums have become dumping grounds for a variety of miscreants and indigents who cannot be dealt with elsewhere, it is seldom acknowledged that asylums were set up with the explicit aim of dealing with such people.

Another particularly compelling example which Szasz gives is of the discovery of an illness termed 'negritude' (1971, pp. 183-9). This illness was discovered by Benjamin Rush (1745-1813), a leading American psychiatrist, following the chance observation of a case of spontaneous cure. Henry Moss was a Negro who in 1792 suffered from a rare skin disease called 'vitiligo' in which white spots appeared on the skin. The case of Moss prompted Rush to suppose that all Negroes were suffering from a mild form of congenital leprosy whose only symptom is blackness. The disease was thought to be hereditary but not contagious. The Negro was, therefore, safe as a domestic, but not as a sexual partner. Thus negritude provided the perfect diagnosis: it upheld the *status quo* and expanded the power of the medical profession. (It is worth noting that Hunter and Macalpine in their collection of extracts from the writings of the history of psychiatry do not include Rush's writing on negritude.) Other examples used by Szasz include the translation of malingering into hysteria by Charcot and the identification of masturbation as the source of a specific variety of insanity. All these examples are used as illustrations of ever expanding medical concerns. They are instances of psychiatric imperialism.

Although Szasz has played a very important part in uncovering a hitherto unsuspected function of psychiatry, his analysis is, I feel, too dogmatic and oversimplified. From a recognition that psychiatry has a social dimension, it does not follow that psychiatrists always act in a way which conserves dominant values and expands the power of the medical profession. The relationship between social values and psychiatry is more varied and complicated than Szasz admits. For example, in the eighteenth century to be diagnosed as suffering from the spleen or vapours was a mark of distinction. David Hume thought he was suffering from the spleen or vapours but was pleased to learn through his correspondence with Dr Cheyne that he had, in fact, contracted 'the disease of the learned'. Thus disease could be used to mark off the top as well as the lower echelons of society. Hysteria, as Robert Burton had pointed out, was the mark of a lady who lived a life of grandeur and idleness. In *The Manufacture of Madness* (1971) Szasz claims that psychiatry protects the rich and well-educated and sets out to expose the psychiatric malpractices which oppress the poor and socially disadvantaged. The direction and purpose of psychiatric oppression as described by Szasz appear uniform and simple. The role of the psychiatrist is that of a 'social tranquillizer' and psychiatric commitment is 'in part a symptom of class struggle'. Behaviour which expresses real and justified grievances is translated into psychiatric language and is thereby robbed of its sting. In *Law, Liberty and Psychiatry* (1974), for example, Szasz cites several famous medico-legal cases of homicide in which insanity was at issue.

> Persons of relatively low social rank openly attacked their superiors. Perhaps their grievances were real and justified and were vented on the contemporary social symbols of authority, the King and Queen. Whether or not these men's grievances justified homicide is not our problem here. I merely wish to suggest that the issue of insanity may have been raised in these trials in order to obscure the social problems which they perhaps intended to dramatize (Szasz, 1974, p.128).

Szasz cites as evidence Hadfield's case in 1800 where the defendant was tried for shooting at George III; Oxford's case in 1840 where the defendant was tried for shooting at Queen Victoria; M'Naghten's case in 1843 where M'Naghten was tried for having shot and killed Drummond, Peel's private secretary. In order to obscure the unwelcome political implications of such attacks, the diagnosis of insanity was introduced. However, this interpretation needs to be queried. It is not at all clear that these attempted homicides involved political considerations in any ordinary sense. The social contribution of psychiatry is a more complicated and varied one than simply disguising political messages.

Hadfield suffered from brain injuries as a result of being wounded in war. He thought that the world was coming to an end and that his assassination of George III would bring about his own desired end. The attempted assassination is to be explained in terms of his own life history and has little meaning outside it. In the case of Oxford's attempt on Queen Victoria's life, the diagnosis of insanity was introduced because of the young queen's tenderheartedness: she was anxious that no one should die on her account. Moreover, two years later when another attempt was made on her life, insanity was not mentioned and the would-be assassin was sentenced to death. With regard to M'Naghten's attempted assassination of Peel, although Peel's period of office was violent and conflict-ridden and political motives for assassination were plentiful, M'Naghten himself does not appear to have been politically motivated. He thought that he was being persecuted by the Jesuits, the Tories and the police and his assassination was an attempt to rid himself of personal suffering. (I am grateful to Professor Harry Herder for his advice on these points.)

In a recent exchange of articles between Thomas Szasz and Martin Roth we find a clear restatement of Szasz's views on the imperialistic nature of psychiatry (1976, pp.317-34). Szasz examines the part played by neurosyphilis in the development of twentieth-century psychiatry. He maintains that the model of syphilis has confused the development of psychiatry for over a century; its investigation has encouraged a trend towards the translation of histopathology into psychopathology. Szasz calls this 'the greatest epistemological translation of our age', by which, of course, he means mistranslation. The model of disease as physical lesion cannot, Szasz claims, be transferred to deviant behaviour in order to provide an account of mental illness. Szasz cites convincing practical reasons why the paradigm of syphilis should have achieved such dominance. Hospital statistics from the early part of this century show that between 20 and 30 per cent of patients were suffering from syphilitic paralysis.[1] Moreover the model of syphilis provided a means of extending the bounds of illness from body to behaviour. Subsequently the growth of institutions created the need for a classification of the behaviour and condition of the inmates of insane asylums: in fact, it led to the elaboration and proliferation of nomenclature. This interpretation is in line with Szasz's view of psychiatrists as imperialists.

At this point it is worth taking stock of the argument since it embodies many typical ingredients as well as weaknesses of Szasz's position. There is an emphasis on the misguided extrapolation from physical to mental illness which is instigated by the craving for power and control of the psychiatric profession. Secondly, those over whom power was exercised in this way were by and large poor and powerless. However, although this view supports Szasz's analysis of the nature of psychiatry, it does not quite fit the facts. Whilst it is true that large numbers of patients in asylums at the end of the last century were suffering from syphilitic paralysis, the consequences which Szasz draws do not necessarily follow: the elaboration and unwarranted proliferation of nomenclature did not take place. Early diagnosis and careful classification as pre-conditions for successful treatment were emphasized by the moral managers in the first half of the nineteenth century. Classification was seen as a necessary prelude to treatment and was meticulously carried out in the period of therapeutic optimism. With the increase in the size of asylums and asylum populations the general standard of care deteriorated. Since cure was no longer a goal, classification was neglected. Thus precisely at a time when the asylum population expanded most rapidly the expected classification of patients did not take place. Hence, one possible technique for furthering medical control was not exploited. Not only that, but those concerned with lunacy, namely asylum superintendents and lunacy commissioners, urged that the asylum should rid itself of the majority of its inmates. Chapter 7 looks in greater detail at the movement from 1844 onwards which urged the return of large numbers of chronic patients to the workhouse. This attempt by the asylum to rid itself of 'incurables' is a reverse of the situation predicted by Szasz's thesis of psychiatric imperialism. With regard to Szasz's claim that the paradigm of syphilis encouraged extrapolation from physical to mental illness, other factors not considered by Szasz contribute towards the merging of physical and mental illness. Firstly, it is worth noting that the view of mental illness as a variety of physical illness antedates the discovery of the syphilitic origin of general paralysis. Henry Maudsley, for example, wrote of the hereditary taint which damns large sections of the British population to a life of lunacy. Most of Maudsley's work was published in the 1870s, whilst the connection between syphilis and general paralysis was only fully established in 1912.[2] It seems more likely that the actual conditions within asylums with ever increasing cases of hopelessly incurable patients promoted a pessimistic view of the nature of madness and its chances of cure. Thus, although Szasz is concerned with the social uses to which psychiatry may and has been put, he is not aware of their variety.

Martin Roth aptly reminds us of the shortcomings of Szasz's principal conceptual device, namely dichotomy (ibid, p.317). Szasz's arguments are developed by means of a series of antitheses: mind is

opposed to body, voluntary action to involuntary, man to society
and psychiatry to law and politics. No room is allowed for ambiguity
or overlap. Roth's example of Parkinson's *Essay on the Shaking
Palsy* (1817) shows the artificiality of Szasz's dichotomies.
Parkinsonism was first described in terms of behavioural not
anatomical abnormalities. Not until shortly before the First World
War were anatomical lesions discovered to account for the
behavioural disturbance. Had Szasz's division between behavioural
deviation and anatomical abnormality been strictly observed, the
discovery of Parkinsonism would have been considerably retarded.
Moreover, there is then the problem of transferring Parkinsonism
from one category, that of non-disease, to another, that of disease.
Others, including sociologists have queried the validity and benefit of
creating such distinct conceptual compartments. For example, Peter
Sedgwick, a political theorist, argues that to divorce mental illness
from 'proper' illness is to ignore the moral and behavioural
dimension of physical illness (Sedgwick, 1972). The existence of
cultural and behavioural variations in the perception and expression
of illness is a commonplace among medical sociologists. Szasz's
exclusive interest in mental illness has meant that he has ignored the
many different ways in which values permeate society.

Andrew Scull is a historian of psychiatry whose PhD thesis
Museums of Madness (1974) provides one of the most challenging
and absorbing accounts of lunacy in the nineteenth century. Chapter
6 on the treatment of the poor is largely concerned with his work. For
that reason it is worth spelling out his position and the ways in which
it differs from mine. Scull sees the separate provision for lunatics in
asylums built for that purpose as inherently problematic. Until the
lunacy reform movement of the early nineteenth century got under
way there was little uniformity in the provision for the insane and
certainly no notion of state responsibility for lunacy. Then, following
a series of parliamentary reports, national conscience was roused and
laws were passed initially recommending and subsequently making
compulsory the building of county asylums. Scull attributes this
change in attitude and policy towards the insane to changes
attendant on the processes of industrialization and urbanization.
With the uprooting of agrarian populations, families were no longer
willing or, indeed, able to look after their disturbed members. The
time was, therefore, ripe for an institutional solution. Thus economic
considerations were responsible for the growth of county asylums:

economically vulnerable families no longer able to support an unproductive and disruptive family member were only too willing to hand over their responsibility to the asylum doctors. At the same time asylum doctors were eager to expand their power and prestige by capturing a group of people over whom they might exercise exclusive authority. Specialization and the growth of professional organizations kept pace with the expansion of the lunatic population. The Association of Medical Officers of Hospitals for the Insane was founded in 1841. In 1853 this association published *The Asylum Journal* which later became *The Journal of Mental Science*. Asylum doctors, influenced by the principles of moral management, urged early detection of illness and in return promised its cure. Clearly the asylum doctors were not just imposing their ideas on an unwilling population; they were responding to very real needs in the community. In the second half of the nineteenth century the asylum went into decline. The asylums grew to unmanageable proportions; despite the therapeutic optimism of the moral managers the number of incurables grew to the extent that asylum superintendents felt that they were being impeded from fulfilling their rightful task. As a policy of despair it was urged that the incurables should either be returned to workhouses or else be sent to other asylums which were run on more economical lines and with no pretence to cure.

In a later book, *Decarceration,* Scull argues that the contemporary community mental health movement, the move to dismantle hospitals or at least to try to keep people out of hospitals and to treat them in the community, is an unexamined position and one which is, in fact, adopted as an economic expedient (Scull, 1977). Scull argues that there is little empirical evidence for the superiority of community treatment as against asylum treatment and that allegiance to community treatment is ideological. The real reasons for the move to community treatment are to be sought neither in revolutionary drug treatment nor in the disrepute into which asylums have fallen, particularly in the writings of sociologists, but rather in economic stringencies. Many large asylums built 150 years ago have reached the end of their life-span unless large sums of money are spent renovating them.

The content of Scull's work will be considered at greater length later; for the present it is worth noting that in both accounts, that is, in the account of the growth of the asylum and in the account of its demise, economic factors are held to be at root. Economic uncertainty among the population at large created the need for asylum care and prompted vast sums of public money to be spent on the erection of asylums. Subsequent unwillingness to spend further public funds on psychiatric care contributed towards the deterioration of treatment and eventually the emptying of asylums. However, this kind of economic determinism does not provide a sufficient explanation. Why were large sums of money spent on the erection of asylums and not on their continued maintenance? Straightforward economic necessity cannot by itself account for changes in economic policy. In fact, a great many factors contributed to the change in the condition of lunacy which took place in the middle of the nineteenth century.

The facts are more complex and less amenable to graphic schematization than as presented by Scull. Parry-Jones has shown that institutional care for the insane was provided on a wide scale throughout the eighteenth century (1972). There were many private madhouses for both private patients and pauper lunatics. General hospitals too contained wings for the insane opened through pressure of public demand and usually run at a loss (private communication from Charles Webster). Thus the nineteenth century did not usher in the beginning of institutionalization, although at this time the need for uniformity of institutional care was most explicitly recognized. However, institutional care as such existed long before the processes of industrialization or urbanization were of any significance. Further explanations, therefore, need to be sought for the growing concern for the plight of the insane. One such factor contributing to the growth of public concern was the illness of George III (1782-1820), who suffered from distinct episodes of what was at the time thought to be insanity. Recent research by Hunter and Macalpine has put forward the argument that George III was, in fact, suffering from a rare metabolic disorder called porphyria (Hunter and Macalpine, 1969). However, be that as it may, public sympathy was alerted to the king's plight because he was thought to be insane and parliamentary inquiries into his condition were set up in 1788 and 1790. The parliamentary reports on the condition of the insane, namely those of 1807 and 1815 coincide with the latter part of his life. Undoubtedly, this purely contingent fact of the king's insanity encouraged lunacy reform. Another source of lunacy reform is to be found in the theory of moral management and the general optimism with regard to insanity and its cure. During the first half of the nineteenth century the ideas of the moral managers dominated psychiatric thought. They held that insanity was independent of physical disease and was to be located in the relationship between the emotions and the will. Precisely because of the location of insanity, man could control the tendency towards insanity by cultivating the will, or, to be more precise, habits of self-control. As I have argued elsewhere, this belief in man's ability to prevent and combat insanity is part of a more general constellation of ideas which invests the individual with great powers of self-control and self-improvement (Skultans, 1975, pp.15-18). It is part of the ideology of the emerging middle classes. The power of belief systems to influence policy is neglected by Scull who sees ideas about madness as an offshoot of economic and social conditions. Furthermore, Scull cannot give an adequate account of changes in policy towards the insane. He describes changes in the attitudes towards the pauper insane and in particular the incurables. Once the asylums were established it was found that the hospital population grew rapidly and that there was an ever increasing demand for beds. However, the asylums were not achieving the cures which they had promised and the number of incurables multiplied. At this point an alternative, cheaper psychiatry was suggested. However, the demand for asylum care and treatment was still there and, indeed, growing and Scull does not make entirely clear why the initial commitment to providing high quality care should have disappeared. Why were the demands for asylum care met at one point in time and not at another? A straightforward economic determinism cannot provide the answers. The weaknesses of Scull's explanations become particularly apparent when we look at his account of the growth of the community mental health movement in this century. Once again the reasons given by Scull for the running down of asylums and the advocacy of treatment within the community are economic. Namely, that asylums now need vast sums of money to be spent on them, and that in the short term community treatment appears to be a cheaper alternative. Economic pressures are used to account for the origin, the deterioration and the disappearance of the asylum. Other factors are thought to be of minimal importance.

Another writer concerned with the history of madness and one whose ideas have achieved great popularity far beyond the speciality of the history of medicine is Michel Foucault. His most widely read book is *Madness and Civilization* first published in England in 1971.

It was originally published in France in 1961 under the title *Histoire de la Folie*. Its connections with the anti-psychiatry movement are suggested both by the choice of David Cooper as author of the introduction and by the wording of the English title. It implies that madness is created by civilization and that in an ideal non-repressive society it would not exist (Foucault, 1971). This is similar to the less intellectually sophisticated nineteenth-century belief that madness increases as civilization advances and becomes more complex. Although this idea of a primeval state of society free from insanity has an intuitive appeal it needs closer examination.

Foucault's work is that of an intellectual and social historian. From the point of view of the history of ideas, Foucault traces attitudes to madness from the Middle Ages onwards. The elementary question which he poses – and which, I feel, he fails to answer – is why was madness set apart and feared? His arguments are roughly as follows: he describes the institution of the Ship of Fools, whereby boats were laden with madmen and cast off to sail from port to port perpetually unwelcome and without home: 'Something new appeared in the landscape of the Renaissance; soon it will occupy a privileged place there: the Ship of Fools, a strange "drunken boat" that glides along the calm rivers of the Rhineland and Flemish canals' (ibid., p.7). After evocative descriptions of the voyages of this mad cargo Foucault asks:

> Why, from the old union of water and madness, was this ship born one day, and on just that day?
> Because it symbolized a great disquiet, suddenly dawning on the horizon of European culture at the end of the Middle Ages. Madness and the madman became major figures, in their ambiguity: menace and mockery, the dizzying unreason of the world, and the feeble ridicule of men (ibid., p.13).

The physical exclusion of madmen and their purification by water is set against the background of disintegrating social structures. Foucault then goes on to consider madness in the classical period:

> In the Renaissance, madness was present everywhere and mingled with every experience by its images or its dangers. During the classical period, madness was shown, but on the other side of bars, if present, it was at a distance, under the eyes of a reason that no longer felt any relation to it and that would not compromise itself by too close a resemblance (ibid., p.70).

A further contrast is drawn between the Renaissance and the classical period: 'Classicism felt a shame in the presence of the inhuman that the Renaissance had never experienced' (ibid., p.68). The characterizations of the experience of madness which Foucault gives are compelling. However, the explanations are not sufficiently discriminating. In an age which glorifies reason, unreason or madness becomes particularly threatening and must be viewed from afar and subjugated. At the level of social and economic history confinement

> marked a decisive event: the moment when madness was
> perceived on the social horizon of poverty, of incapacity for
> work, of inability to integrate within the group; the moment
> when madness began to rank among the problems of the city
> (ibid., p.64).

Elsewhere Foucault writes

> throughout Europe, confinement had the same meaning, at least
> if we consider its origin. It constituted one of the answers
> the seventeenth century gave to an economic crisis that
> affected the entire western world: reduction of wages,
> unemployment, scarcity of coin (ibid., p.49).

Leaving to one side the vexed issue of whether there was a significant deterioration in economic conditions which provoked the 'great confinement', it is interesting that Foucault has very similar explanations for both the Renaissance and the classical treatment of madness.

At the beginning of the nineteenth century the outrage at the plight of the insane is interpreted as a fear that they may contaminate other confined individuals who were not insane: 'The presence of the mad appears as an injustice; but for others' (ibid., p.228). And 'If the mad defile those with whom they have been imprudently confined, a special internment must be reserved for them; a confinement that is not medical, but that ought to be the most efficacious and the easiest form of aid' (ibid., p.236). The moral managers are not credited with having liberated the insane, rather they are seen as having instituted a more complete, because psychological, form of control.

> The terror that once reigned was the most visible sign of the
> alienation of madness in the classical period; fear was now

endowed with a power of disalienation, which permitted it to
restore a primitive complicity between the madman and the man
of reason. It re-established a solidarity between them. Now
madness would never – could never – cause fear again; it would
be afraid, without recourse or return, thus entirely in the
hands of the pedagogy of good sense, of truth and of morality
(ibid., p.244).

The professed intentions of the moral managers are ignored or 're-
evaluated'.

We must therefore re-evaluate the meanings assigned to
Tuke's work: liberation of the insane, abolition of constraint,
constitution of a human milieu – these are only
justifications. The real operations were different. In fact Tuke
created an asylum where he substituted for the free terror of
madness the shifting anguish of responsibility; fear no longer
reigned on the other side of the prison gates it now raged
under the seals of conscience (ibid., p.247).

In short, Foucault claims that 'the absence of constraint in the
nineteenth-century asylum is not unreason liberated, but madness
long since mastered' (ibid., p.252). What the moral managers claim
they are doing is not what they are really doing. Foucault's reinterpretation of their action fits his general theory even though it
may not accord with the moral managers' ideas of what they are
about. In conclusion, Foucault does not pay sufficient attention to
the intentions and explanations of the actors themselves but imposes
his own schematic arguments deriving from his particular pre-
conceptions. Throughout his book Foucault holds the implicit
assumption that society has not been able to enter into a genuine
dialogue with madness (whatever that would involve) and that
treatment of madness at any age is an expression of fear and an
attempt to either banish or control.

   Although this book does not set out to be a chronological record of
events the chapters are ordered roughly in chronological sequence.
(An attempt at a more complete chronology is provided by the table
of dates, p.146.) Chapter 2 describes ideas on melancholy and
madness current in the sixteenth and seventeenth centuries. At that
time the term melancholy was a catch-all for many complaints as the
comprehensiveness of Burton's work on melancholy testifies

(Burton, 1621). In particular, a melancholic disposition was seen as a sign of unusual gifts and sensibility. It is not surprising that Burton is prepared to publicly confess his affliction if melancholic men are 'of deep reach and excellent apprehension'. Chapter 3 explores writing on the spleen and hypochondriasis, otherwise known as the English Malady. The spleen is heir to melancholy taking over as a catch-all for many vague nervous and physical discomforts. It is thought to affect the English in particular, hence the title of George Cheyne's book *The English Malady* (1734). Chapter 4 looks at the ideas and practices of the moral managers in the early part of the nineteenth century. The moral managers set out to discard the old methods of physical treatment and control and instead aimed at restoring the will-power of the patient, hence their name. Physical restraint and physical treatments such as blood-letting were abandoned in favour of gentle persuasion in a family-like setting. Chapter 5 examines the appearance in the mid-nineteenth century of a new disease called masturbational insanity. Although little interest had been shown in masturbation and the activity had certainly not been thought to have any medical relevance, the 1830s and 1840s witnessed a spate of books on the grave medical consequences of masturbation. Chapter 6 describes ideas about feminine nature and examines the way in which feminine character was thought to set women at greater risk of insanity. A woman's reproductive role and her more emotional nature were thought to increase female vulnerability to nervous disorders. Throughout history women have been attributed with what amounts to a constitutional proneness to insanity. Chapter 7 describes the parliamentary reform movement and the growth of county asylums. The problems of lunacy were closely related to those of pauperism, in that a considerable number of lunatics came under the authority of the Poor Law. Once asylums were established they rapidly increased in size and it is difficult to establish whether this was because of an increase in the number of lunatics or the number of indigents. The final chapter is concerned with the notion of hereditary insanity particularly as it appears in the work of Henry Maudsley. At the same time as asylums were filling up with cases of incurable pauper lunatics, physicians like Maudsley were concerned to demonstrate the part played by heredity in producing a class of hopeless moral degenerates. Maudsley's writing is no longer concerned with cure but with the identification and demarcation of the mentally unsound.

Note

[1]Szasz's figures for the numbers of patients suffering from syphilis must be treated with caution. Nineteenth-century diagnostic practice is notoriously unreliable and the figures for the numbers of syphilitic patients are no less so than those for other diagnoses or the number of cures. They tell us more about the theoretical outlook of the diagnosticians than they do about the patients themselves.

[2]The clinical features of general paralysis had been described in 1822 by Antoine Bayle in Paris. During the latter half of the nineteenth century sexual excess and alcoholism were thought to be associated with general paralysis, so much so that Krafft-Ebing coined the phrase 'Civilisation and syphilization' in 1897. However, spirochaetes were only identified in paretic brain sections by Noguchi in 1912, and the growing suspicion of the relation between syphilis and general paralysis was finally confirmed (for a fuller discussion of this topic, see Hare, 1959).

2
Elizabethan melancholy

The history of psychiatry presents the reader with many contradictions. Beliefs often conflict with practice and different sets of beliefs often coexist during the same period. For example, nineteenth-century writers on insanity advocated enlightened treatment, yet there are numerous denouncements of the care which they provided and accusations of unjust confinement. The problem is no less intractable earlier in history. In particular, we find the recurrence of this double aspect of insanity. On the one hand it is seen from a subjective point of view as a potentially universal affliction. (This is the viewpoint later advocated by the nineteenth-century moral managers who urged abandonment of restraint and advocated appeal to the individual's conscience. Insanity in their view could be overcome, if not prevented, by the exercise of will-power and the cultivation of character.) On the other hand, insanity is seen as part of a gothic landscape of doom and terror, synonymous with bestiality – it forms a configuration of which confinement is a necessary part.

Elizabethan concepts of madness are also contradictory. The background to most writing about illness at this time is the theory of the four humours. Humoural pathology is based on pre-Socratic ideas about the nature of the cosmos. According to Empedocles the universe consisted of four elements: earth, air, fire and water. These elements give rise to four basic qualities, namely, coldness, dryness, hotness and wetness. Within the body these qualities appear as the four humours, namely, the spleen, blood, choler and phlegm. It is the predominance and particular combination of humours which determines a person's temperament; the balance and imbalance determines health and disease. Within this general framework accounts of more specific illnesses are developed. For example, writers of the period distinguish so many subcategories of melancholy that it almost seems as though Renaissance psychopathology regards all mental abnormality as a species of melancholy. Roughly speaking, our term madness is synonymous with the Elizabethan term melancholy.

One of the earliest discussions of nervous disorders is to be found in Timothy Bright's *Treatise of Melancholy* (1586). Here melancholy is thought to be caused either by humoural imbalance or by divine retribution as the following passages testify:

> If the spleneticke excrement surcharge the bodie, not being
> purged by helpe of the splene: then are these perturbations
> far more outrageous, and harde to be mitigated by counsell or
> persuasion (ibid., p.109).

And

> Although no man is by nature freed from this affliction in so
> much as all men are sinners and being culpable of the breech
> of God's laws, incurre the punishment of condemnations
> yet is the melancholicke person more than any subject
> thereunto. . . (ibid., pp.198-9).

This combination of humoural and theological explanation is characteristic of much writing of the period, including Robert Burton's massive work on melancholy. Thomas Wright introduces a different theme in that he discusses the part played by the emotions in causing illness:

> Passions cause many maladies, and well nigh all are increased
> by them, for all that pain engendereth melancholy, which for
> the most part, nourisheth all diseases: for many we reade of that
> were cured by mirth, but never any by sorrow or heavinesse
> (Wright, 1604, p.63).

The impossibility of a perfect reconciliation of the passions is evocatively described:

> Sometimes you shall have a number of greedy Passions like so
> many young crowes halfe starved gaping and crying for food,
> every one more earnest than another to be satisfied; to content

them all is impossible, to content none is intolerable to
prosecute one and abandon the rest, is to carry so many hungry
vipers gnawing upon the heart strings of the soule (ibid., p.73).

Long before Freud the balance between reason and instinct was
recognized as being precarious.

The best known and most popular of the treatises on melancholy
is, no doubt, *The Anatomy of Melancholy* by Robert Burton (1621,
11th edition 1806). Burton describes his success with the book: 'The
first, second and third edition were suddenly gone, eagerly read'
(ibid., p.27). In this encyclopedic work Burton enumerates and
describes the symptoms of melancholy but declines to give a
definition of the affliction.

Proteus himself is not so diverse; you may as well make the *Moon*
a new coat, as a true character of a melancholy man; as soon
find the motion of a bird in the air as the heart of a melancholy
man (ibid., p.469).

However, amid the long lists of types of melancholy can be discerned
two underlying approaches. These two faces of melancholy were
never really reconciled within a single expository tradition.
Melancholy is used as both a medical and psychological term – a
usage which reflects the contemporary mind/body problem.
Although the body is earthly and the soul divine – the two are knit
together by spirit which BUrton says is like 'a true love knot, to
couple heaven and earth together'. THus melancholy becomes a
simultaneous affliction of body and soul.

Between 1500 and 1580 there are only three references to
melancholy in English plays. After 1580 references to melancholy
suddenly proliferate – so much so that writers have been led to speak
of an 'epidemic' of melancholy. For example, Lawrence Babb writes:
'an epidemic broke out apparently about 1580, and continued for
several decades. For some time melancholy men were so numerous in
London that they constituted a social type, often called the
malcontent' (Babb, 1959, p.3). This affliction was explained
according to either the authority of Galen or of Aristotle. The
Galenic tradition represents the melancholic man as suffering from
an excess of black bile, 'a heavy viscid humour, so thick and adhesive
that physicians have great difficulty in evacuating it and the mental
conditions which it engenders are accordingly highly tenacious'

(Babb, 1951, p.57). The seat of melancholy or black bile is the spleen – an organ which acquired increasing importance in the eighteenth century. According to the Galenic tradition the melancholy man is 'morose, taciturn, waspish, misanthropic, solitary, fond of darkness. He commonly suffers from grotesque hallucinations. He is extremely wretched and often longs for death' (Babb, 1959, p.3).

The Aristotelian tradition, on the other hand, associates melancholy with poetic inspiration and wit. The original question attributed to Aristotle is: 'Why is it that all those who have become eminent in philosophy or politics or poetry or the arts are clearly of an atrabilious temperament and some of them to such an extent as to be affected by diseases caused by black bile?' (Aristotle, 1927, p.953a). Burton is following this tradition when he describes melancholy men as 'of a deep reach, excellent apprehension, judicious wise and witty' (ibid., p.451). Timothy Bright in his treatise on melancholy also follows this tradition. He writes that if the humour: 'be attenuated with heate it delivereth a drie subtile and piercing spirit, more constant and stable than any other humour, which is a great help to this contemplation' (Bright, 1586, p.130). Du Laurens also views melancholy in a favourable light. He writes that melancholy under propitious circumstances: 'causeth as it were, a kind of divine ravishment, commonly called *Enthousiasma,* which stirreth one up to plaie the philosophers, poets, and also to prophesie: in such manner as it may seem to containe in it some divine parts'. However, certain conceptions contrive to fuse the Galenic and Aristotelian tradition: 'The malcontent's harsh, unpleasing and eccentric exterior, then is in the Galenic tradition. This unprepossessing exterior, however, is supposed to veil great interior excellence. The malcontent is – or thinks he is – a person of unusual intellectual and artistic talent' (Babb, 1951, p.76).

How can we account for this resuscitation of the Aristotelian view of melancholy. One simple, if somewhat superficial explanation lies in the increase in foreign travel. Some scholars have claimed that the vogue for melancholy was brought back from Italy by fashionable young travellers. Furthermore, the aristocratic origins of the affliction would encourage its spread. 'Since the imitative travellers were ordinarily young gentlemen, melancholy for a time at least had aristocratic connotations in Elizabethan England, and these made the pose doubly attractive' (Babb, 1951, p.74). According to this conception melancholy serves as a mask to superior beings who find that life does not come up to their expectations. *The Anatomy of Melancholy* makes explicit mention of disguise and role-playing as an ingredient of melancholy. Burton says that playing of parts and building castles in the air is one of the most pleasurable aspects of the early stages of melancholy. These qualities of melancholy are embodied in Hamlet: 'Hamlet's role-playing conveys what lies behind the melancholic's traditional attributes of shrewdness and secrecy – his sense of a hostile world that makes him unwilling to divulge his identity to others' (Lyons, 1971, p.110). In fact, the entire *Anatomy* can be regarded as an exercise in role playing or *melancholizing.* Burton himself appears under the pseudonym Democritus Junior, 'the intelligent, detached and reflective onlooker who must laugh with Democritus lest he weep with Heraclitus. The role is assumed, but by no means foreign to Burton's actual personality' (Babb, 1959, p.37).

What explanations are there for the epidemic of melancholy – apart from its fashionableness and aristocratic connections? First, the connection between a scholarly life and melancholy had general currency. Second, many educated men of literary talents found great difficulty in earning a livelihood for themselves. For example, studies of the literary profession in Elizabethan England have shown the increasing deficiencies of the old system of patronage and the lack of new alternatives. Phoebe Shearyn writes:

> The plain fact was that the demands on patronage were too
> heavy to be met. The system was breaking down under
> changed conditions. In medieval times, if patrons were few so
> were writers, and there were accepted refuges for writers in noble
> and monastic houses (Shearyn, 1909, p.20).

Needless to say, such refuges no longer existed during the period under consideration. And, as evidence of the inadequacy of patronage, Shearyn cites the following: 'It is a sure sign of lack of effective patronage when an author dedicates his works to a great variety of patrons' (ibid., p.23) – as so often happened during the sixteenth and seventeenth centuries. The social and economic sources of melancholy are also emphasized by Lindsey Knights in her book *Drama and Society in the Age of Jonson.* She writes:

> Under James I, in each rank of society, there were men who by
> character and education were fitted, or considered themselves

fitted, for a higher position than they were able to obtain. Under Elizabeth there had been a considerable increase of educational activity, with a consequent heightening of men's expectations. Even before the close of the sixteenth century there were more than a few who could find no definite place in the existing organization of the state, and with the coming of the Stuarts and the ending of the war with Spain, many more felt themselves capable of undertaking tasks which they saw in the hands of favourites and jobbers (Knights, 1937, p.324).

The period was a difficult one for men of talent and sensibility who felt that their individual merits were unrecognized and were passed over unrewarded. 'Contemporaries were well aware of the danger of over-education and thwarted ambition'. In fact, Lindsey Knights claims that the connection between poverty and melancholy was so frequently made as to be a music-hall joke.

Finally the vogue for the melancholy pose reflected the general temper of the age (see, for example, Allen, 1938; Williamson, 1935). Harrison, introducing Breton's *Melancholike Humours,* writes: 'At most periods it is the isolated mood of an individual out of tune with his sphere; in the generation preceding *The Anatomy* it was the prevailing mood with intelligent writers' (Breton, 1929, p.49). With the astronomical studies of the sixteenth century, ancient ideas of the mutability and decay of the world were revived. Ambition was out of place in a world which was approaching its end. Certainly the melancholic role was viewed as an appropriate and desirable one for the well-travelled and world-weary scholar. In contrast to the elevating potential of the melancholic stance, the cult of enthusiasm which appeared in England in the seventeenth century provided the opportunity for using allegations of madness as a method of vilification and degradation of certain religious groups.[1]

However, there is another aspect of melancholy which has not yet been examined. Accounts of it are less easy to come by; writers are less willing to acknowledge it as theirs. It does appear in Elizabethan drama where madness/melancholy and its cure are frequent topics of conversation. In literature we find both the acceptable face of melancholy readily espoused by refined and sensitive individuals, and the more sinister, unacceptable face of melancholy bordering on madness. For example, Rosalind in *As You Like It* compares love to 'a madness' which 'deserves as well a dark house and a whip as madmen do' *(As You Like It,* III, ii, 420). Romeo alludes to slow starvation as a cure for madness:

> Benvolio: Why Romeo art thou mad?
> Romeo: Not mad, but bound more than a madman is, Shut up in prison, kept without my food, Whipped and tormented *(Romeo and Juliet,* I, ii, 154).

A character from Marston's *What You Will* has a charmingly business-like response to madness: 'Shut the windows, darken the room, fetch whips; the fellow is mad, he raves, he raves – talks idly – lunatic.' The madhouse has become a 'house of correction to whip us into our senses' (Shirley: *Bird in a Cage,* II, 1). Shakespeare's view summarizes that of the asylum keeper:[2]

> Diseases desperate grown
> By desperate appliances are relieved
> Or not at all.

To summarize, under the same term melancholy we find two quite differently perceived conditions, treated in quite different ways. The one aspect invites exploration; the other, although familiar to popular imagination, is feared and treated by chaining, whipping and stripes. Such a corrosive and destructive humour, despite its frequency, is little known.

This dichotomy in ideas continues into the eighteenth century. The distinction is clearly made by Dr Johnson. Boswell writes of their conversation:

> Dr Johnson and I had a serious conversation by ourselves on melancholy and madness; which he was, I always thought, erroneously inclined to confound together. Melancholy, like 'great wit' may be 'near allied to madness', but there is, in my opinion, a distinct separation between them. When he talked of madness, he was to be understood as speaking of those who were in any great degree disturbed, as it is commonly expressed, 'troubled in mind'. Some ancient philosophers held, that all deviations from right reason were madness; and whoever wishes to see the opinions both of ancients and moderns upon this subject, collected and illustrated with a variety of curious facts, may read Dr Arnold's very entertaining work (Johnson is referring to *Observations on*

Madness, vol. l, 1782; vol. ll, 1806. For a further discussion of Johnson's ideas on madness see chapter 3.)

It seems there is a residuum of psychological disorder which is disowned even by those writers who are very much at home in the inward-looking world of nervous distempers. This total rejection of madness means that the possibility of publicly exploring it and discussing it, is precluded. The only possibility left is physical subjugation. Not surprisingly, this approach led to the barbarous treatment of the inmates of asylums and of the solitary lunatic.

Notes
[1] From the mid-seventeenth century onwards a number of religious sects developed which emphasized the immediacy of the relationship between man and God. Inner feeling was thought to be the best guide to God's truth. From our viewpoint it is interesting that this religious development gave rise to a school of psychiatric literature which argued that certain religious groups which relied on religious enthusiasm were, in fact, mad. Between the mid-seventeenth and mid-eighteenth centuries a large number of treatises with such titles as *A Discourse Proving that the Apostles were no Enthusiasts* (Campbell, 1730), *A Short View of the Pretended Spirit of Prophesy* (Hutchinson, 1708), and *A Treatise Concerning Enthusiasme, As it is an effect of Nature: but is mistaken by many for either divine Inspiration, or Diabolical Possession* (Casaubon, 1655). These writers argue that the supposed intimations of heaven are nothing more than disturbed states of body and mind. In fact, the religious claims of the enthusiasts are treated with a considerable amount of derision. Hutchinson, for example, writes:

> How commonly do we find our methodists full-swelled with vanity and pride, boastings, haughtiness and arrogance? In a little time they feel a *compunction;* the bladder is pricked, shrinks and shrivels and they fall into the most lonely and abject state of vileness and nothingness (1708, p.98).

The claims of the religious enthusiasts provide an object lesson to others not to give free rein to the imagination and not to treat feeling too seriously:

> For such high pretenders having renounced the government of reason, and given up themselves to their own fancy and imagination without any fixed principles that can bound them, and being accustomed to feel some very warm emotions upon their minds that are always apprehended to come immediately from heaven. . . . (Campbell, 1730, p.9).

Here we have an early attempt to disqualify experience by describing it as pathological. George Rosen considers radical sects in a wide-ranging, comparative article called *Emotion and Sensibility in Ages of Anxiety* (1967b). Rosen is interested in the interface between 'the public issues of social structure' and 'the personal troubles of milieu', in particular in the way in which rapid social change produces anxious individuals.

Ages or periods of anxiety are ones when the social and moral framework of a society, or of a group within it, crumbles – when the world seems out of joint. At such times the tension between outer experience and the world within, between social reality and emotional disarray, leads to the development of a type of sensibility and an emotional climate dominated by anxiety (Rosen, 1967b, pp. 773-4).

Frequently this anxiety results in allegations of insanity. The example of seventeenth-century religious sects shows the way in which alternative and threatening forms of religious experience have sometimes been treated. The technique must be all too familiar to twentieth-century readers.

[2] I am indebted for these examples to Edgar Allison Peers's *Elizabethan Drama and its Mad Folk*, 1914, London, Heffer, pp. 28-9.

3
The English malady

English susceptibility to nervous disorders

The last chapter described the considerable hostile literature on enthusiasm and its connection with madness which persisted into the eighteenth century. By the middle of the century an earlier theme had reappeared – melancholy. One literary critic wrote:

> No characteristic of English poetry in the mid-eighteenth century is more familiar to students of the period than the perpetual reference to melancholy . . . whatever one's opinion of the intrinsic merit of this versified melancholy or of its genuineness as an expression of personal feeling, there can be no dispute over its quantity. Statistically this deserves to be called the Age of Melancholy (Moore, 1953, p.179).

He goes on to point out that no cult can flourish unless it is rooted in popular experience. The mood of melancholy was, therefore, a familiar experience; moreover, its prevalence was remarked upon by foreign visitors. As it spread, melancholy acquired many new names: the spleen, vapours, hypochondriasis, hysteric fits, the hyp and finally and most aptly the 'English malady'. John Purcell published a *Treatise of Vapours and Hysteric Fits* (1702) in which he claimed that this condition was the most common English ailment. Bernard Mandeville, less well known as a nervous specialist, decided to settle in London precisely on that account. The English malady was restricted to literate, if not literary circles. However, it is worth remembering that alongside the fashionable nervous ailments there existed Bedlam and many other houses of confinement where inmates were treated as a strange animal-like species.

Foreign travellers in England invariably commented on English susceptibility to melancholy. The foreigner's view of English proneness to this state is described by Cecil A. Moore (1953). He refers to George Luis Le Sage who, in an account of his stay in England, wrote: 'Surely, the people of England are the most unhappy people on the face of the earth – with liberty, property and three meals a day.' Another observer of English character was the Abbé Prévost, founder of the periodical *Pour et Contre* (1733-40). This magazine attracted its readers largely by regaling them with accounts of 'les extravagances anglaises'. The Abbé Le Blanc spent seven years in England and wrote both about the English upper classes and about country people:

> However, in the midst of this plenty, we easily perceive that the farmer is not so gay here, as in France, so that he may perhaps be richer, without being happier. The English of all ranks have that melancholy air, which makes part of their national character. The farmers here show very little mirth, even in their drunkeness; whereas in France, the farmers in several provinces drink nothing but water, and yet they are as gay as possible (quoted in Moore, 1953, pp. 183-4).

In view of this predisposition to melancholy it seemed strange to the Abbé Prévost that the English should have no equivalent to the French word *ennuie*. Instead the English terms are 'feeble substitutes' such as spleen and vapours. Conversely the French language could not adequately express the meaning conveyed by the words spleen or vapours. This is borne out by the fact that the word spleen passed officially into French usage in 1798. This was defined by the Academy as 'ennuie de toutes choses maladie hypochondriaque propre aux Anglais'.

However, this characterization of the English as beset by nervous troubles was not just an expression of malice on the part of their neighbours. The English themselves vaunted their proneness to nervous disorders. The pages of the *Tatler* and the *Spectator* carry numerous references to the splenetic nature of the English. Steele wrote of the 'innate sulleness or stubborness of complexion' of the English *(Tatler, no. 213)*. Addison wrote of melancholy as 'a kind of demon that haunts the island' *(Spectator, no. 387)*. Horace Walpole believed that English men were least able to endure solitude. In 1777 Boswell wrote: 'I flatter myself that the hypochondriack may be agreeably received as a periodical essayist in England where the malady known by the denomination of melancholy, hypochondria, spleen or vapours has long been supposed to be universal' (1951, p.23).

Social differences and nervous disorders

In the medical literature the earlier generic term was melancholy which provided a catch-all for ailments of the mind and body. Melancholy appeared under several names. One of the effects of this proliferation of nomenclature was to provide a means of establishing the social status of sufferers. People of quality suffered from the spleen, their servants were afflicted by lowness of spirit. But like all fashions, diseases too descended the rungs of the social ladder. Moore, in the previously quoted article, makes the dubious point that although the upper classes did not differ physiologically from their 'inferiors', they were more vulnerable to what are now called neuroses and psychoses on account of their luxurious and idle life style (Moore, 1953, p.189). Both these claims can be disputed. It is likely that the upper classes enjoyed a definite physiological advantage over the working classes, despite their excesses. Furthermore, all recent research on mental illness indicates that physical suffering does not provide immunity from mental suffering – on the contrary – it contributes towards it. However, since specialists in nervous disorders were by and large a luxury which only the rich could afford, we have little record of the poor. Diseases also distinguished between the sexes as well as taking social differences into account. From the highest ranks downwards, women were peculiarly susceptible to emotional disorders. Queen Anne, for example, suffered from multiple afflictions and, therefore, provided a model for other women to imitate. John Purcell had argued that the spleen had a particular 'gusto for the tender sex' (1702). Indeed, most of the eighteenth-century specialists depended for their livelihood upon the custom of ladies of quality. However, although women were acknowledged to suffer from the spleen, more often this appeared in a peculiarly feminine manifestation, namely, as hysteria. The Greeks had regarded hysteria as a feminine disorder by definition. Sydenham, on the other hand, thought that hysteria was but a feminine counterpart of the *passio splenetica*. In other words, when the spleen or melancholy occurred in women it was diagnosed as hysteria. Browne argues that women are peculiarly susceptible to the spleen since they are literally the weaker sex:

> for since a weak and lax state of the solids is essential to this disorder, as is evident from the symptoms; and since in the fair sex, a peculiar Weakness, Tenderness and Delicacy is observable in the frame and texture of their fibres: it may with just Reason be supposed, that hence it is that they are more liable to this Disease (1729, pp.71-2).

The vapours was another sex-linked term which was initially assigned only to women and then spread to men.

Signs and symptoms of the spleen

A further attempt to distinguish the varieties of spleen was made by Nicholas Robinson in *A New System of the Spleen, Vapours and Hypochondriack Melancholy* (1729). He subdivided the spleen according to its duration: stage 1 he called the spleen or vapours; stage 2 he called hypochondriac melancholy; stage 3 he called melancholy; stage 4 he called madness. Such was thought to be the natural history of the disease. Sir Richard Blackmore was yet another physician interested in the spleen. His *Treatise of the Spleen and Vapours* was published in 1725 and he was physician to the splenetic Queen Anne. However, he was also a poet of considerable ambition and he did not confine his interest in the spleen to medical textbooks. In his turgid poem *Creation* there is a digression on the spleen:

> The spleen with sullen vapours clouds the brain,
> And binds the spirits in its heavy chain,
> However the cause fantastic may appear,
> The effect is real and the pain sincere.

Much of the writing fostered a valetudinarian, if not hypochondriacal outlook. Symptoms which did not fall neatly into a diagnosis were referred to this rag-bag. The anonymous author of *A Treatise on the Dismal Effects of Low-Spiritedness* (1750) was afraid that his readers might not be sufficiently sensitive to the dangers of the spleen. Stukeley in his book *Of the Spleen* (1723) enumerates a massive list of symptoms for which to look out:

When the head is attack'd, coma's, epilepsy, apoplexy, or the
numbness of a part ensue, or talkativeness, tremors, spasms,
headach; when the heart palpitations, swooning anxiety;
when the breast, sighing, short-breath, cough; when the
diaphragm, laughing; when the belly (and more frequently
being the seat of the morbid minera) rugitus, cardialgia, colic,
iliac passion etc. (ibid., p.70).

In short, the spleen was a hydra-headed monster that could spring
upon the unwary in any one of a myriad, unsuspected forms. This
difficulty of detection was enhanced by the fact that, according to Dr
Thomas Dover, the spleen could imitate other physical ailments. In
this characteristic, it was rather like the nineteenth-century view of
hysteria which was thought to counterfeit the symptoms of
neurological disorders. Small wonder that terror of the spleen was
widespread and confusion so great. Queen Anne's physician, John
Arbuthnot, described the spleen as 'a disease more terrible than
death' and its symptoms as:

obstinate watchfulness, or short sleeps, troublesome and
terrible dreams, great solicitude and anxiety of mind, with
sighing, sudden fits of anger without any occasion given, love
of solitude, obstinacy in defending trifling opinions and
contempt of such as are about them, suppression of usual
evacuations, as of the menses in women and haemorrhoids in
men; great heat, eyes hollow and fixed, immoderate laughter or
crying without occasion; too great loquacity, and too great
taciturnity, by fits; great attention to one object, all these
symptoms without a fever (1756, pp.374-5).

The spleen was, therefore, aptly called the protean disease. Not
surprisingly it encouraged a growth in the number of physicians and
permitted a diversity of medical opinion. The eighteenth century has
become known as the age of quackery when physicians were subject
to the greatest amount of ridicule and scorn. Fielding and Smollett
were among the literary men who took the medical profession to task
on the score of quackery.

The spleen and suicide
However, although writers might mock doctors, the public were
terrified of the effects of the spleen and, indeed, of its final outcome –

suicide. The prevalence of suicide was thought to be high enough in England as to constitute a national scandal. An article in *Mercurius Politicus* maintained that more people killed themselves in England than in all the other countries of the world put together. The real or supposed epidemic of suicide led to the appearance of a considerable literature on the rightness and wrongness of suicide. In the twenty-sixth of his *Lettres persanes* (1721) Montesquieu offered an apology for suicide. The letters were translated into English the following year and were widely read. They received an anonymous reply in the form of a tract entitled *Queries concerning Self-Murder offered to a gentleman in distress* (1741), and David Hume added a chapter on suicide and immortality to the 1757 edition of his *Essays Concerning Human Understanding*. Although he subsequently withdrew this addendum, it nevertheless first appeared in uncorrected form. Montesquieu claimed that the English killed themselves in the very lap of fortune and happiness. Voltaire, as well as supposing that the direction of the wind had some connection with suicide, thought that Englishmen killed themselves in order that their name might appear in print: they were concerned with posthumous notoriety.

Exact statistical information on the numbers of suicides is not available; what we do have are descriptions of the general state of mind and the publicity given to particular acts of suicide. During the year 1755, according to Thomas Gray, self-murder was 'epidemical'. Read's *Weekly Journal* (22 December 1755) estimates the number of known suicides for that year at 47, and the number 'found dead' at 26. These numbers are not large by any standards. The epidemic proportions of suicide come not so much from the numbers of dead as from their notoriety and the fears which these suicides engendered. The epidemic was first set in motion when Lord Mountford killed himself after gambling away his estate at White's Chocolate House. This incident and the subsequent suicide of a fellow-clubman filled the newspapers for many weeks. The alarm excited by these events was due to the social position of the suicides and the part these events played in popular imagination.

Explanations of the spleen

How did the physicians cope with this general terror of the spleen and its dreadful outcome? What explanations and remedies were available? For the most part explanations were couched in physical terms. Cheyne, for example, wrote:

> I never saw a person labour under severe, obstinate, and strong
> nervous complaints, but I always found at last, the stomach,
> guts, liver, spleen, mesentery or some of the great and
> necessary organs or glands of the belly were obstructed,
> knotted, schirrous, spoiled or perhaps all these together (1734,
> p.184).

Blackmore attributes the spleen to 'the peculiar constitution of the
air . . . or the immoderate quantity of flesh meats they eat, or the malt
liquors they drink or any other secret causes. . .' (1725). And it is, of
course, true that in the history of gastronomy the eighteenth century
witnessed great excesses. George Cheyne in his *Essay of Health and
Long Life* divides the book into the following chapters: Of air; of
meat and drink; of sleeping and watching; of exercise and quiet; of
our evacuations and their obstructions; of the passions. Each chapter
heading is the name of a so-called non-natural and taken together the
six non-naturals were thought to provide a complete aetiology of
disease.[1] Any one or a combination of the non-naturals was thought
to cause disease. The two non-naturals most frequently cited as
causes of disease are the excessive eating and drinking habits and the
pathogenic climate. Indeed, Cheyne makes specific reference to these
two non-naturals in the opening sentence of his treatise on the
English Malady (1734). He writes:

> The title I have chosen for this treatise, is a reproach
> universally thrown on this island by foreigners, and all our
> neighbours on the continent, by whom nervous distempers,
> spleen, vapours, and lowness of spirits are in derision called
> the English Malady. And I wish there were not good grounds
> for this reflection. The moisture of our air, the variableness of
> our weather, (from our situation amidst the ocean), the
> rankness and fertility of our soil, the richness and heaviness of
> our food, the wealth and abundance of our inhabitants (from
> their universal trade) the inactivity and sedentary occupations
> of the better sort (among whom this evil mostly rages) and the
> humour of living in great, populous and consequently
> unhealthy towns, have brought forth a class and set of
> distempers, with atrocious and frightful symptoms, scarce
> known to our ancestors, and never rising to such fatal heights,
> nor afflicting such numbers in any other known nation. These

nervous disorders being computed to make almost one third
of the complaints of the people of condition of England
(ibid., pp.I-II). (Note again the significant social restrictions
placed upon the prevalence of the disorder.)

Similar weight is attached to diet and climate by John Brown in his
Estimate of the Manners and Principles of the Times (1757). Nine
years later Brown provided proof for his theories by taking his own
life. Moore summarizes the eighteenth-century views: 'the
inhabitants of England were doomed by geographic accident to be a
melancholy people' (1953, p.210). Foreigners had a similar opinion
of the injurious effects of the British climate. Moore writes of the
Abbé Le Blanc:

> As a scientist he takes it to be a self-evident truth that human
> beings, no less than vegetables, partake of the nature of the
> climate that produce them. From the same natural conditions
> proceed the fertility of the British soil and that melancholy
> disposition of the inhabitants which makes.it impossible for
> them to submit to political or religious regimentation or to
> endure the ordinary misfortunes of existence (ibid., p.212).

Although at first the English argued against the evil nature of their
climate and its effects on the population, they eventually resigned
themselves to the foreigners' view of themselves 'and once they had
accepted the ugly truth, they dwelt with martyr-like zeal upon their
foul climate and its depressive influence' (ibid., p.213). Lady Mary
Wortley Montagu who spent a large part of her life outside England
complained bitterly of the English climate. She writes in one of her
letters: ''tis necessary to have a very uncommon constitution not to be
tainted with the distemper of our climate.' Thus there were
overwhelming physical reasons why the English could not escape the
spleen.

**Scientific background to medical ideas: Hydraulic and vibrational
theories**
What was the scientific background against which these ideas were
developed? Until the seventeenth century medical thought was
dominated by humoural pathology. The balance and imbalance of
the humours was thought to determine health and disease. Although

humoural explanations persisted until well into the nineteenth century, by the seventeenth century they no longer enjoyed a monopoly. Explanations in terms of forms and qualities were partly superseded by a mechanical philosophy whose key concepts were matter and motion. Descartes provided a complete version of mechanical philosophy. Harvey successfully embodied these mechanical precepts in his discovery of the circulation of the blood. However, even when mechanical concepts had replaced humoural explanations within medicine, animal spirits lived on. In Descartes's philosophy they provided the mediating link between mind and body. Intangible, yet not entirely spiritual, they tried to hold together a theory which did not quite cohere. As applied to medicine the animal spirits provided agents of nervous communication. Whereas, before the action of animal spirits could be impeded by humoural imbalance or by viscid or corrosive humours, with the advent of mechanical theory the animal spirits were described in terms of configurations of particles. If they were uneven or protuberant they could become lodged in inappropriate parts of the body.

Another source of inspiration for explaining the nervous system was hydraulics. Nervous communication was seen as analogous to the circulation of the blood. These ideas originated from Boerhaave who argued that the nerves were the finest of the body's tubules and that nervous fluid flowed along them which was made up of the finest of bodily particles. The state of the nervous fluid and, in particular, the quality of its motion, determined health and disease. Regularity of motion of the nervous fluids was desired and irregularity of nervous motion was thought to be the source of nervous distempers. In many ways the hydraulic view of the nervous system was similar to Galenic explanations in terms of animal spirits. Only the terminology appears to have changed. Whereas earlier Galenic physicians had referred to disordered movements of the animal spirits, the disorder was now located in the movement of the nervous fluid.

The structural similarity of these explanatory theories facilitated the replacement of one theory by the other. Moreover, the new theory was constructed around a simple graphic model and was, therefore, easy to visualize. The hydraulic model of the nervous system consisted of two basic elements: the containing pipes and the contained fluid. Although microscopic studies might have suggested this particular view of the nervous system, they could neither confirm nor negate it. It remained speculative and was retained for reasons that were not entirely empirical. Variations on this basic scheme could be developed by changing the emphasis on the contained or containing elements. Cheyne saw the body as a complex network of tubes and fluids. These fluids might become sluggish and clogged and hence lead to the spleen if the wrong diet were followed and luxurious habits indulged. Hence, wrong diet was the cause of disease and the right kind of food was the remedy for ill-health. Indeed, in both *The English Malady* (1734) and *An Essay of Health and Long Life* (1724) Cheyne advocates a regimen of milk and vegetables. Given the inordinate quantities of meat which were consumed by the rich of the period, this may well have been sensible, if unwelcome, advice. Cheyne is particularly eloquent on the evil effects of alcohol:

> The truth is, all fermenting juices, such as these eminently are, must be highly injurious to weak constitutions; for meeting with the crudities in the bowels, they must raise a new battle and coluctation there, and so must blow up the whole cavities of the human body, with acrid fumes and vapours, the great and sore enemy of such bowels (Cheyne, 1724, p.57).

The account is suffused with a sense of high drama. However, Cheyne's prescriptions for treatment embodied a number of theoretical outlooks as the following extract shows:

> But the fundamental proposition on which the manner of treating such distempers is, and ought in reason to be grounded, and which experience alway justifies, is that a laxity, weakness and want of due tone and elasticity in the solids, produce viscid, sharp, and ill-conditioned juices. And, on the contrary, that ill-conditioned, sharp and viscid juices, necessarily produce weak and unelastic solids, so that they mutually exasperate each other, and differ only as cause and effect, though the fault of the fluids always precedes that of the solids. Put the case that the blood and juices are viscid, sharp and ill-conditioned, the fibres subsisting nearly in their proper tension and due degree of tone and elasticity, that they ought to be in perfectly sound and robust persons, the necessary effect of such a state of juices, would be a retardment of their circulation by a greater pressure of the sides of the vessels, and the forming of obstructions in the small and capillary tubes, which by rendering these impervious,

forces a greater quantity upon the pervious ones, than they are accustomed or able to drive about, and so by degrees break and loosen the texture and relax the tone of all these solids (Cheyne, 1734, p.106).

A fusion of conceptual systems is comfortably maintained by Cheyne. The passage just quoted contains elements of vibrational theory which provided a further theoretical framework for physicians. According to this theory, bodily health was thought to depend on its tone or elasticity. Too much tension of bodily fibres as well as too great a flaccidity was the source of nervous ill-health. Nicholas Robinson gave an account of nervous communications in terms of fibrous tension and elasticity (1729, pp.16-18, 111-112). Cheyne, being very much an eclectic, combined the hydraulic and vibrational system. The vibrational theory was derived ultimately from Locke and his theory of sensations. However, the use to which vibrational theory was put by physicians was very different from that of the association psychologists. Tense nervous fibres provided a metaphor for nervous malaise. Thus, throughout the eighteenth century a fundamental concern was the discovery of the bodily concomitants of nervous malaise.

Philosophical approaches to madness

The most frequently cited authors on madness in the eighteenth century are Foucault and Rosen. Both writers consider the dominant philosophical ideas of the period. Foucault argues that during the Renaissance and, in fact, until the seventeenth-century madmen lived alongside their sane fellows, madness was an ever-present force which was not excluded from everyday life. However, with the coming of the Age of Reason, madness or unreason acquired a particularly threatening power. An age which glorified reason and saw it as man's most important attribute could only deal with unreason by total exclusion. Hence, the physical exclusion of lunatics and what Foucault terms the grand confinement took place. Rosen argues that the eighteenth century saw

a change in the social perception of irrationality and madness based on criteria derived from a new view of human nature. Today, the idea of a personal self appears as an indispensable assumption of existence. Actually, like other views of human nature, it is in large measure a cultural idea, a fact within

history, the product of a given era. At any given period certain
criteria are employed to establish normal human nature,
as well as any deviation from it (Rosen, 1963, p.233).

Reason and self-reflection provided the defining characteristics of
man. Rosen cites Pascal who could conceive of a man without hands,
feet, a head, but claimed 'I cannot conceive of a man without
thought; that would be a stone or a brute' (quoted in Rosen, 1963,
p.234). Similarly, for Descartes thought provided the Archimedean
point for his entire philosophy. Another characteristic which Rosen
cites as essential to the eighteenth-century outlook is a sense of
appropriateness and tact. Rosen examines the French terms
honnêteté and *bienséance*. He writes:

> Rules of social conduct mingled with axioms of morality and
> notions of social prudity to provide a standard by which all
> unseemly depths of emotion were concealed and extravagances
> of behaviour avoided. In these terms when accepted values and
> desires are carried to extremes, they appear in an illegitimate
> and utterly repellent form. A person who acts in this way cuts
> the lines of communication between himself and other men,
> thus becoming less than human (ibid., p.235).

Rosen goes on to say that these values provided the cultural
background for the *Grand Siècle*. Although there were some
comparable developments in late seventeenth-century England, the
idea of social fittingness acquired a strong foothold in England
somewhat later. Ideas of what constitutes gentlemanliness
dominated behaviour. Chesterfield's admonition to his son: 'It is not
good to go against nature, but neither is it good to show too much
nature', epitomizes this attitude. From this social matrix sprang the
institutions for dealing with irrational behaviour: 'Their creation was
the product of a social order, characterized by certain dominant
attitudes' (ibid., p.240).

These accounts of irrationality proceed from a consideration of
the dominant ideas and values of the period. A different account
emerges from a direct consideration of the medical writings on the
spleen. However, although the perspectives are different, they need
not be incompatible. One account places madness within medical
theory, the other shows why its manifestation was so threatening.
Recent studies of the presentation of madness in eighteenth-century

literature also provide the intellectual background to ideas about madness. Two such American studies are *Nightmares and Hobbyhorses* (Deporte, 1974) and *Visits to Bedlam* (Byrd, 1974). Deporte begins with a description of Bedlam and its many visitors. He explains its popularity as follows:

> Indeed, it should not surprise us in an age where satire and lampoon flourished, where nonconformity in religion or politics was bitterly resented and attacked, and where 'politeness' was so highly esteemed, that the madman should exercise particular fascination from taste and good sense (ibid., p.3).

Visitors were charged a penny a visit and for this they could tease the inmates to their hearts' content. Deporte cites a recent estimate which puts the number of visitors at 96,000. He describes the many barbarous and cruel treatments to which patients were subjected: heads were routinely shaved and blistered; patients were dropped without warning into freezing water; routine medical treatments were dramatic – purging, bleeding and vomiting. However, such barbaric treatment of the insane cannot be explained by the contemporary medical views on insanity. Deporte seems to imply, although he does not say so outright, that explanations of madness as due to an imbalance or corruption of the body's humours inclined towards the vicious treatment of the insane. In fact, of course, it does no such thing. To assume that treatment depends upon the particular theory of madness is to subscribe to a naive physical determinism. In fact, with the exception of moral management, treatments remained remarkably constant even though theories of madness changed completely. For example, blood-letting was practised until well into the twentieth century for very different theoretical reasons.

Deporte's summary of the work of eighteenth-century nervous specialists is unflattering. He refers to the fact that writers seldom give actual case histories to illustrate their theories, but repeat case histories given by earlier writers. Cheyne is an exception, but Deporte discounts his case histories because he claims they relate to physical illness. This is not a fair assessment because Cheyne believed the spleen to have so many physical manifestations. Be that as it may, Deporte concludes that 'the theories of eighteenth-century physicians are speculative in the worst sense: they are spun from a few inaccurate hypotheses, and are so unrelated to observed fact that they are not even educated guesses' (1974, p.11). He does, however, concede that these theories embodied a knack for metaphor and analogy. This metaphorical quality is present in most eighteenth-century writing, giving it its dramatic force and making it easy to visualize. It is not surprising that many of the eighteenth-century medical writers also had literary interests. Bernard Mandeville wrote *A Treatise of the Hypochondriak and Hysterick Passions* (1711) and also *Poem of the Fable of the Bees* (1724). Sir Richard Blackmore was known for his *Treatise of the Spleen* (1725) as well as his epic poetry. Indeed, he is among the poets who figure in Samuel Johnson's *Lives of the English Poets*. Deporte aptly points out that with Blackmore in particular 'the language of his epics seems, at times, interchangeable with the language of his medical works' (ibid., p.11). Although Cheyne had no literary pretensions the same could be said of his descriptions of the disorders of the gut – they have the dramatic quality of epic poetry. Moreover Cheyne has the advantage of a terseness and pithiness of style which the long-winded Blackmore lacks. For example, Cheyne makes a very telling statement about his relationship with his rather grand clientele. He complains that 'fine folks use their physicians as they do their laundresses, send their linen to them for it only to be dirtied again' (Cheyne, 1724, p.182). And more poignantly perhaps: 'The spirit of man can bear his infirmities, but a wounded spirit who can bear?' (Cheyne, 1734, p.1). The line between medicine and literature is a fine one at this period.

Medical writing has a literary tone. Conversely, the theme of madness is pursued throughout eighteenth-century literature. The literary treatment of madness develops one particular strand of the medical literature. It looks at the passions, the sixth of the non-naturals responsible for causing the spleen. Ideas about the role of the passions in causing disease stem from faculty psychology. According to it, men possessed three souls: the rational, the sensitive and the vegetative soul. The vegetative soul is concerned with involuntary functions such as growth, nutrition and reproduction; the rational soul is concerned with understanding and the will; the sensitive soul is concerned with imagination, memory and perception. Mental health depends upon the relationship between the rational and the sensitive soul, that is between the will and understanding and the imagination and passions. To allow too much importance to the imagination was thought to endanger health.

Thomas Wright in an early treatise described the evil effects of unrestrained passions as: 'blindness of understanding, persuasion of will, alteration of humours; and by them maladies and diseases, and troublesomeness and disquietness of the soul' (1604, p.47). This fear of the evil effects of imagination, although it is a powerful and constant theme in the eighteenth-century literature, has its source in the previous century. The theme is continued and developed in the eighteenth century alongside other explanations of madness.

Johnson on madness

Foremost among the distrusters of imagination is Samuel Johnson, who spent a lifetime struggling against melancholy and the horrors of an over-active imagination. He was for ever on his guard against the temptations of the imagination, although he did recognize its palliative force. In one instance he wrote: 'Life is a bitter pill which none of us can bear without too much gilding: yet for the poor we delight in stripping it still barer.' Yet too much gilding had fearful consequences. A biographer writes of Johnson's life-long effort directed towards 'controlling an over-powerful imagination, in resisting melancholia, [which] left him at times with a will exhausted because overtaxed' (Wain, 1974, p.67). And later Johnson is described as suffering from a 'Hamlet-like paralysis of the will' (ibid., p.67). In conversation with Fanny Burney, Johnson is said to have recommended the usefulness of seeing a madhouse from one's window:

> It is right that we should be kept in mind of madness, which is occasioned by too much indulgence of imagination. I think a very moral use may be made of these near buildings: I would have those who have heated imaginations live there and take warning (1958, pp.1225-6).

Johnson's fear of imagination lies precisely in the fact that it is so tempting and because reality is, by contrast, so drab and uninteresting; reality is bound by restrictions, whereas fantasy is without limitations:

> The dreamer retires to his apartment, shuts out the care and interruptions of mankind, and abandons himself to his own fancy; new worlds rise up before him, one image is followed by another,

and a long succession of delights dances him. He is at last called back to life by nature, or by custom and enters peevish into society, because he cannot model it to his own will (*Rambler,* no. 89).

Moreover, the connection between imagination and madness is close as Imlac explains in Johnson's novel *Rasselas*:

the mind dances from scene to scene, unites all pleasures in all combinations, and riots into lights which nature and fortune with all their bounty, cannot bestow. In time some particular train of ideas fixes the attention, all other gratifications are rejected, the mind in weariness or leisure recurs constantly to the favourite conception, and feasts on the luscious falsehood whenever she is offended by the bitterness of truth. By degrees the reign of fancy is confirmed, she grows first imperious, and in time despotic. Then fictions begin to operate as realities, false opinions fasten upon the mind, and life passes in dreams of rapture or of anguish (*Works,* London, I, pp.293-4).

Because of the constant temptations presented by imagination Johnson writes: 'Of the uncertainties of our present state the most dreadful and alarming is the uncertain continuance of reason.'

Johnson's ideas on melancholy are echoed by Boswell in his essays published under the pseudonym the Hypochondriack. Boswell claims that melancholy is universal and thereby queries the familiar Aristotelian association between madness and genius:

I must with all due respect to Aristotle, beg leave to doubt the proposition, that it is peculiarly to be found in men of remarkable excellence. And I think it is of importance that the proposition should not be believed – because I am certain that many who might have prevented the disease from coming to any height, had they checked its first appearances, have not only not resisted it, but have truly cherished it, from the erroneous flattering notion that they were making sure of the undoubted though painful characteristic of excellence. . . (Boswell, 1951, p.43).

The disease should not be allowed to gather strength but should be crushed with 'all possible speed' (ibid., p.44). However, in the case of this particular disease such a course is particularly difficult since 'Nothing characterises a Hypochondriack more peculiarly than irresolution, or the want of power over his own mind' (ibid., p.47). Irresolution or lack of power of the will is what Johnson most deplored in himself and Boswell is clearly modelling his ideas about hypochondria on his knowledge of Johnson's suffering.

Johnson's attitude to madness was fundamentally different from that of the earlier Augustan satirists. Johnson's attitude is one of compassion and identification not the derisory mocking attitude of Swift or Pope. According to Boswell, Johnson visited Bethlem Hospital on a number of occasions. However, the spirit of his visits was different from that of earlier visitors. As Byrd writes:

> Madness is not for Johnson the indispensable metaphor of folly, error or malice that it was for Pope and his contemporaries. Neither the emblem of a dunce nor the just punishment of a villain, it here became a human (but not a superhuman) affliction (Byrd, 1974, p.96).

Byrd contrasts this with Swift's preoccupation with madness:

> never in all the complicated shiftings of perspective in *A Tale of a Tub* are we intended to identify ourselves fully with the mad narrator, his insanity is too spectacularly outrageous to accept as our own; and even when he calls the world mad and invites it into a bedlam cell, we understand him to be talking about the foolish, irrational world, not our well-behaved world, normal and reasonable (ibid., p.96).

In complete contrast Johnson writes about madness from personal experience and warns us of solitude which 'is dangerous to reason, without being favourable to virtue... Remember... that the solitary mortal is certainly luxurious, probably superstitious and possibly mad: the mind stagnates for want of employment, grows morbid and is extinguished like a candle in foul air' (ibid., p.98). Imagination for Johnson is closely allied to sin and slothfulness:

> My indolence since my last reception of the sacrament has sunk into grosser sluggishness and my dissipation spread into wilder negligence. My thoughts have been clouded with sensuality, and, except that from the beginning of this year I have in some measure forborn excess of strong drink my appetites have predominated over my reason. A kind of strong oblivion has overspread me, so that I know not what has

become of the last year, and perceive that incidents and
intelligence pass over me without leaving any impression.
This is not the life to which heaven is promised. I propose
to approach the altar again tomorrow (entry 4, 21 April 1764
in Johnson, 1958).

The recurring contrast between drab reality and the temptations of
imagination is made again. Interestingly, idleness is condemned not
because of its supposed connection with poverty, but because of the
inner decay which it promotes. Again, unlike Pope and Swift,
Johnson is not concerned with the public aspects of madness, his
concern is with the hidden, inner madness which may be invisible to
others. However, Johnson was quite open about his own
indisposition. He admits: 'I inherited, (said he,) a vile melancholy
from my father, which has made me mad all my life, at least not
sober' (Boswell, 1961, p.302).

Katherine Balderston in a perceptive article argues that Johnson's
generalizations about madness stem from his personal suffering.
And she argues convincingly that Johnson's fear of imagination
betrays a fear of his masochistic sexual fantasies about Mrs Thrale.
These fears became so unbearable to Johnson that he asked Mrs
Thrale to restrain him physically and put a padlock and chain on
him. Clearly Johnson is speaking from the heart when he says to
Boswell: '"A madman loves to be with people whom he fears not as a
dog fears the lash; but of whom he stands in awe" I was struck with
the justice of this observation. . .' He added

Madmen are all sensual in the lower stages of the distemper.
They are eager for gratification to sooth their minds and divert
their attention from the misery which they suffer: but when
they grow very ill, pleasure is too weak for them, and they seek
for pain. Employment, Sir, and hardships prevent melancholy.
I suppose in all our army in America there was not one man
who went mad (1792-1888, vol. II, p.21).

Balderston claims that this is a commentary on his own case.

The Augustans and madness

Johnson's sympathetic and fearful approach to madness is far
removed from Pope's condemnation: 'The native anarchy of the

mind is that state which precedes the time of reasons assuming the rule of the passions.' Pope's Dunces evoke revulsion in the reader and like the Yahoos in *Gulliver's Travels,* they revel in excremental obscenities. Throughout the *Dunciad* the gulf between madness and truth is emphasized. This emphasis is made with the help of two images, first enthusiasm, in particular religious enthusiasm, and, second, dreaming. Both are seen as clouding reason. This approach to madness is exemplified in Ned Ward's descriptions of the inmates of Bedlam. One inmate is described as follows:

> At last he counterfeits a sneeze, and shot such a mouthful of bread and cheese amongst us, that every spectator had some share of his kindness, which made us retreat; some went back to hear what he had to say, and he had provided them a plentiful bowl of piss, which he cast very successfully amongst them, crying in a laugh, I never give victuals, but I give drink, and you're welcome gentlemen (quoted in Byrd, 1974, p.18).

Another description of an inmate illustrates the equation between madness and delusion:

> We peeped into another room where a fellow was hard at work as if he's been treading mortar. 'What is it, friend,' said I, 'thou art taking all this pains about?' He answered me thus, still continuing in action: 'I am trampling down conscience under my feet, lest he should rise up and fly in my face. Have a care he doesn't fright thee, for he looks like the devil and is as fierce as a lion, but that I keep him muzzled. Therefore, get thee gone or I will set him upon thee.' Then he fell a-clapping his hands, and cried, 'Halloo, halloo, halloo, halloo, halloo,' and thus we left him raving (Ward, 1704, p.54).

The description of these two inmates of Bedlam illustrate the two main aspects of the Augustan view of madness. One is the animal-like quality of madness and its identification with excrement, and the other is its deluded, irrational quality. Second, no sympathy is wasted between spectator and madman. This attitude contrasts both with earlier and later attitudes. The precise explanation of this shift in attitude is difficult to determine. In his perceptive discussion of Augustan ideas of madness, Byrd suggests 'the confusion that private values always bring to public order'. By this threat to public order he means development of religious nonconformity.

The religious enthusiast, for example, so closely bound up with the political conflicts of the earlier seventeenth century, even without a political role would have come to seem dangerous somehow to humanistic values. In his madness he had, after all, dispensed with the older priority of reason and trusted instead to private voices and visions unverifiable by other men; and as with every madman his privacy suggested subversion (Byrd, 1974, p.53).

Another, more general explanation is to be found in the importance attached to public knowledge and this stems from the epistemological tradition established by Locke. Byrd sums up the Augustan age: 'We can hear writers speaking out, anxiously and pessimistically, against the meanings of madness; by the end of the century we hear the authentic voice of the madman speaking for himself' (ibid., p.57).

Swift's ideas about madness are very similar to those of Pope. In some *Thoughts on Free-Thinking* he argues that thoughts 'ought to be kept under the strictest regulation' (Swift, 1939 edn, IV, p.49). And he claims that the difference between a madman and a sane person is

That the former spoke out whatever came into his mind, and just in the confused manner as his imagination presented the ideas. The latter only expressed such thoughts, as his judgement directed him to choose, leaving the rest to die away in his memory (ibid., p.49).

The divorce between imagination and reason is ever present and the distrust of imagination continues strong. The horror of lunacy and its equation with everything base is also present:

A lunatic is, indeed, sometimes merry, but the merry lunatic is never kind; his sport is always mischief; and mischief is rather aggravated than atoned by wantonness; his disposition is always evil in proportion to the height of his frenzy; and upon this occasion it may be remarked, that if every approach is a deviation to ill, every deviation to ill may be considered as an approach to madness *(The Adventurer,* no. 88, 8 September 1753).

Another theme is the association between madness and excrement:

Nor wonder how I lost my wits;
Oh! Caelia, Caelia, Caelia shits.

In *A Tale of the Tub* these ideas about madness are given dramatic expression. In particular Swift expresses his fear of religious enthusiasm and excess:

> All of the associations that the Augustans habitually attached to madness – poverty, idleness, bestiality, disorder, excrement – stand out like so many wounds upon Swift's enemies; and the condition of madness transcends one place to become ironically (but not comically) the human condition (Byrd, 1974, p.79).

At a personal level Swift was both a hypochondriac and a valetudinarian. Swift has been described as 'at times almost morbidly preoccupied with health and disease' (Wilson, 1964, p.199). His self-characterization as 'a stranger to the spleen' was wishful thinking rather than truth. The eighteenth century is known as the age of quackery and Swift was foremost in denouncing it as such. His personal experience of doctors was extensive and at the age of seventy Swift said that 'he esteemed many of them as learned and ingenious men but that he never received the least benefit from their advice or prescriptions' (ibid., p.212).

Locke and madness

The philosophical background to ideas about madness is derived from John Locke. In *An Essay on Human Understanding* Locke aims to find the true basis of knowledge and part of this concern involves being able to give an account of false beliefs and, specifically, disorders of the mind. Locke distinguishes between madmen and idiots as follows

> In fine the defect in naturals, seems to proceed from want of quickness, activity, and motion, in the intellectual faculties, whereby they are deprived of reason, whereas madmen, on the other side, seem to suffer by the other extreme. For they do not appear to me to have lost the faculty of reasoning, but having joined together some ideas very wrongly they mistake them for truths . . . as though incoherent ideas have been cemented together so powerfully as to remain united. But there are degrees of madness, as of folly; the disorderly jumbling

ideas together in some more in some less. In short herein seems to lie the difference between idiots and madmen. That madmen put wrong ideas together, and so make wrong propositions but argue and reason right from them. But idiots make very few. or no propositions, but argue and reason scarce at all (Hoeldtke, quoted in 1967, p.47).

Emphasis on errors in the association of ideas meant that 'madness was a disease of ideas rather than a disease of men' (ibid., p.47). Locke goes on to describe the effects of a distortion in the association of ideas:

The wrong connection in our minds of ideas in themselves, loose and independent one of another has such an influence, and is of so great a force to set us awry in our actions, as well moral as natural, passions, reasonings and notions themselves, that perhaps there is not any one thing that deserves more to be looked after. . . . When this combination is settled and whilst it lasts, it is not in the power of reason to help us, and relieve us from the effects of it (quoted in ibid., p.47).

David Hartley, a later associationist philosopher, argues that madness is caused by unnatural associations which in turn are the product of excessive vibrations:

Suppose a person, whose nervous system is disordered, to turn his thoughts accidentally to some barely possible good or evil. If the nervous disorder should fall in with this, it increases the vibrations belonging to its ideas so much, as to give it a reality, a connection with self. For we distinguish the recollection and anticipation of things relating to ourselves, from those relating to other persons, chiefly by the difference of strength in the vibrations and in their coalescences with each other. . . If an opposite state of body and mind can be introduced early, before the unnatural associations are too much cemented, the madness is cured: if otherwise, it will remain, though the bodily and mental cause should be at last removed (Hartley, 1801).

Here we find a mixture of current medical ideas with philosophical ones. Hoeldtke points out that the ideas of Locke and Hartley had little influence at the time they were written and that any influence they did have was only fully felt a century later. 'Early eighteenth century physicians could not easily accept the whole complex scheme of this new school of thought, for they could understand neither Locke's abstract psychology, nor Hartley's bizarre vibrational theory' (ibid., p.48). This statement is more true of Locke's ideas than it is of Hartley's which were incorporated into much medical writing on the spleen.

Returning to Locke's ideas, it is interesting to note that he does not implicate reason in madness but rather imagination. Madmen

> do not appear to have lost the faculty of reasoning but having joined together some ideas very wrongly, they mistake them for truths, and they err as men do that argue right from wrong principles. For by the violence of their imaginations, having taken their fancies for realities, they make right deductions from them (Locke, 1959, p.209).

The sanctity of reason is thus preserved and the familiar division between reason and imagination is maintained. This is a development of Burton's ideas who said that 'madness is first in imagination and afterwards in reason' (quoted in Deporte, 1974, p.20). However, although the division between imagination and reason is a familiar one, the role assigned to imagination is a novel one. Deporte writes: 'It is education and environment, rather than fear, lust or rage which warp the imagination and deceive reason' (ibid., p.23). And he concludes that: 'By minimizing the role of passion and stressing the importance of education, Locke in effect removes mental disease from the province of the moralist' (ibid., p.23). Whether this is, in fact, the case is debatable, since Locke's ideas have definite deterministic implications. A more obvious interpretation and likely consequence of Locke's ideas on madness is that since madness consists of wrongly associated ideas and since ideas are based on perceptions, the roots of madness are to be sought partly within the environment and partly in faulty processes of association. According to this account madness is treatable by manipulation of the environment and the correction of ideas. In fact, this formed the basis of treatment for the moral managers (see chapter 4).

Examples of eighteenth-century practice

How did particular physicians practise? George Cheyne (1673-1743) was a fashionable physician although his place in medical history is insignificant. He was born in Aberdeen and practised in London and Bath and attended to many famous and aristocratic patients. An essay on the life of Cheyne (Viets, 1949, pp.435-52) claims that Cheyne's success and importance lies in advocacy of 'the value of the temperate life in an intemperate age and thus [he] set an example of what we might call today the austere way of life' (p.435). Many of Cheyne's ideas about the spleen were derived from personal suffering. From boyhood onwards he suffered from nervousness: 'Upon the slightest excesses, I always find slippery bowels . . . an early shaking of my hands and a disposition to be easily ruffled on a surprise' (ibid., p.439). Cheyne abandoned his original intention to enter the Church and instead studied medicine at Edinburgh under Pitcairn. After publishing *A New Theory of Fevers* (1701) an honorary degree was conferred upon Cheyne from Aberdeen.

> Mr George Cheyne allowed to be graduate doctor in medicine gratis, because he's not only our countryman, and at present not rich, but is recommended by the ablest and most learned Physicians in Edinburgh as one of the best mathematicians in Europe; and for his skill in medicine he hath given a sufficient of that by his learned tractat *De Febribus,* which hath made him famous abroad as well as at home; and he being just now going to England upon invitation of some of the members of the Royal Society (ibid., p.441).

Cheyne arrived in London in the winter of 1701 and was promptly elected a member of the Royal Society. Viets describes him as 'serious, ambitious and argumentative'. However, Cheyne soon fell into dissolute company and this had deleterious consequences for his health as he himself records in *The English Malady* (1734). He writes:

> Upon my coming to London, I all of a sudden changed my whole manner of living; I found the bottle-companions, the younger gentry, and free-livers, to be the most easy of access and most quickly susceptible of friendship and acquaintance, nothing being necessary for that purpose, but to be able to eat lustily, and swallow down much liquor; and being naturally of a large size, a cheerful temper and tolerable lively imagination, and having, in my country retirement, laid in store of ideas and facts, by these qualifications I soon became carressed by

them, and grew daily in bulk, and in friendship with these gay
gentlemen and their acquaintances: I was tempted to continue
this course, no doubt, from a likeing as well as to face a trade,
which method I had observed to succeed with some others and
thus constantly dining and supping in Taverns, and in the
houses of my acquaintances of taste and delicacy, my health
was in a few years brought into great distress by so sudden and
violent a change. I grew excessively fat, short breathed,
lethargic and listless (Cheyne, 1734, p.326).

Cheyne found that his symptoms got worse and that he suffered from
a 'constant violent headache, giddiness, lowness, anxiety and terror,
so that I went about like a malefactor condemned' (ibid., p.327). In
order to regain his health Cheyne retired to the country where he
took vomits and purges and lived on a frugal diet abstaining from
meat and alcohol. When this bodily and spiritual crisis descended
upon him, he found that he was 'forsaken by my holiday friends, and
my body was, as it were, melting away like a snowball in summer'.
Throughout his long life he suffered, with intermissions in this way.
His sufferings were so extreme that he claims he can 'scarce describe
or reflect on them without horror' (ibid., p.346). But by constant
discipline and 'a milk, seed and a vegetable diet, with proper
evacuations' he was able to control his illness (ibid., p.352).

There is little record of Cheyne's early years in London, but by the
time of his breakdown in 1715 at the age of forty-two he was well-
known and had a flourishing practice. Among his patients were
Samuel Johnson, John Wesley, David Hume, Beau Nash and the
Countess of Huntington. Although Cheyne left no mark on the
scientific development of medicine, his fashionable and
distinguished practice clearly demonstrates the high esteem in which
he was held.

Another physician whose career parallels that of Cheyne is Tobias
Smollett (1721-1771). He too had a practice in London and was preoccupied above all with his own health. He wrote: 'I have had a
hospital these fourteen years within myself and studied my own case
with the most painful attention'. Like Cheyne, Smollett attributed
his disease to lack of exercise: 'my disorder first arose from a
sedentary life, producing a relaxation of the fibres, which naturally
brought on a listlessness, indolence, and dejection of the spirits'
(quoted by Musher, 1967, p.458). Another cause of the relaxation of
fibres was the pathogenic climate of England.

The overall impression of mental health in England in the eighteenth century is bleak. In his essay, Cheyne admits that the English live longer than other nationals, 'yet scarce anyone, especially those of the better sort, but becomes crazy, and suffers under some chronicle distemper or other, before they arrive at old age' (1724, p.181). This accounts for the high incidence of suicide, since according to Cheyne 'all self-murderers are first distracted and distempered in their intellectual faculties' (ibid.).

Note

[1] Cheyne's classification led Lawrence Sterne to speculate why the most natural things in the world should be called non-naturals by Cheyne.

4
The moral managers

The role of the emotions

Throughout the eighteenth century the emotions had represented the animal in man and were to be subjected. Psychology advocated the extinction of the passions. By the end of the century this position had been totally reassessed. This change in attitude has been carefully examined in an essay by Kathleen Grange (1962, pp.512-23). Her essay is constructed around the analysis of a metaphor – a ship symbol 'which man has consistently chosen to depict his psychological predicament' (ibid., p.512). She traces the development of this metaphor from the philosophy of the Stoics onwards. For the Stoics the duty of the pilot was to bring his vessel into harbour. Tranquillity was the most sought after condition. This, of course, is opposed to the Aristotelian position which allies madness with genius and more generally sees emotion as a spur to action. This Aristotelian line of thought was developed by Thomas Wright in his *Treatise of the Passions in Generalle* (1604). Wright argues that emotions, rather than being impediments, play a necessary part in stirring us to action. Henry More argued that emotions purify the blood. 'Boyle, La Rochefoucauld and More thus minimised the danger of storm, in opposition to the stoics, they maintained that the brisk winds of emotion served as active forces guarding man's vessel from quicksands, stagnation and inertia' (Grange, p.517). This approach culminated in the romantic cultivation of feeling. Absence of emotion was tantamount to death. Kathleen Grange finds this romantic approach epitomized in the poetry of Coleridge: 'In place of stagnant calm, he suggested the need for humanitarianism and for the cultivation of feeling, mood and emotion' (ibid., p.522).

Changes in attitudes to the emotions are reflected in attitudes to sleep. Byrd describes the changed attitudes to sleep from Augustan suspicion to romantic interest in its creative possibilities.

> Creative madness for poets like Wordsworth, Byron and Coleridge actually stands for that self-renewing retreat from ordinary reality (often to the underworld) which figures so prominently in the romance cycle. Where Pope and Swift turned to the image of madness to express the extent and danger of a destructive dullness, the romantic writers use the same image to communicate a sense of frustrated human possibilities – possibilities often frustrated in their view by exactly those Augustan pressures of community (Byrd, 1974, p.149).

And Byrd talks of 'the stock romantic figure, the poet haunted by his own genius' (ibid., p.157). Blake's ideas are of special importance. He believed that inspiration is necessarily associated with madness in the eyes of the world, a belief echoed by Laing almost two centuries later. This is a far cry from Johnson's terror-stricken and dejected stance towards his emotional suffering.

Pinel's influence

This reappraisal of the contribution of emotions to man's health and happiness also influenced attitudes to insanity. Although this book is about madness in England some attention must be paid to the ideas of Pinel in order that development in psychiatric theory and practice may be more completely understood. Pinel's dramatic gesture in freeing the patients at the Salpêtrière and the Bicêtre of their chains has become legendary. Aubrey Lewis starts his essay on Philippe Pinel and the English by saying that 'Pinel is remembered today because he showed that cruelty and neglect play no part except a shameful one in the care of the mentally ill' (Lewis, 1955, p.581). Lewis goes on to argue that 'Pinel received more from England than England received from him' (ibid., p.584). However, although the influence was reciprocal and Pinel translated Cullen's *Institute of Medicine,* his influence on the practice of psychiatry in England was undoubtedly enormous. In 1806 a translation of his *Traité* was first published in England and his influence on the non-restraint movement and the moral managers can be dated from that time.

Among those influenced by Pinel are Samuel Tuke, Robert Gardiner Hill and John Conolly.

As far as the theory of insanity was concerned, Pinel continued to attach importance to the emotions. Kathleen Grange points out that: 'From 1690 to 1800 psychology was considered to be an account of the intellectual operations of the mind' (1961, p.444). However, Pinel was not primarily interested in the analysis of such functions as memory, perception and will, but rather in the analysis of the emotions. This activity was termed 'moral' as opposed to intellectual study. Kathleen Grange writes: 'for Pinel and his school insanity was to be cured by opposing and balancing the passions' (ibid., p.452). A wider reading of Pinel and the moral managers shows that the emphasis should be on balance of the passions rather than opposition to them. The inmates of the large asylums were freed precisely because Pinel felt that their passions could be regulated and trusted. In fact, liberty was a condition of cure: 'a limited liberty in the interior of the hospital, allowing him all the movements of non-dangerous effervescence' (*Traité*, 2nd edn, p.262, Woods and Carlson, 1961, p.22). Pinel's attention to the emotional element in mental illness involves a departure from Locke's rational conception of insanity. In his descriptions of mania without delirium Pinel identifies his differences from Locke.

On resuming at Bicêtre my researches into this disorder, I thought with the above author, that it was inseparable from delirium; and I was not a little surprised to find many maniacs who at no period gave any evidence of any lesion of the understanding, but who were under the dominion of instinctive and abstract fury, as if the active faculties alone sustained the injury (quoted in Kavka, 1949, p.462).

Pinel's theoretical outlook permitted him to identify new categories of mental illness.

This leads on to a further important aspect of Pinel's work – his emphasis on empirical observation. The eighteenth century, it will be remembered, was a period of much speculation in the field of nervous illnesses. Theories were adopted for their metaphorical and visual aptness rather than on the basis of empirical fact. By contrast Pinel's approach was cautious and empirical. He was not interested in formulating a comprehensive theory of disease. He was interested in 'only those symptoms and signs which are recognisable by the senses and which are not susceptible to vague reasoning' (quoted in Woods and Carlson, 1961).

Changes in treatment

It has often been said that lunatics were not treated as a separate type of deviant and lunacy was not regarded as a separate category before the late eighteenth century (see, for example, Scull, 1974; Jones, 1972; Foucault, 1971). This contention needs to be examined more closely. Andrew Scull argues that the rise of the asylum and with it the medicalization of madness rests on 'the primitive stirrings of urbanisation and industrialisation' (Scull, 1974, p.46). With the growth of large towns, families were no longer able to look after their incapacitated members. Urban living magnified the scale of problems and made earlier methods of relief seem outmoded. However, Scull also claims that earlier explanations of madness had been theological or demonological. Physicians had made virtually no impact on the understanding of insanity. Scull writes: 'For much of the first half of the eighteenth century, James Monro (1680-1752), the physician at Bethlem, was almost the only doctor in and around London who treated the mentally ill' (1974, p.63). Although this claim fits in with the view that insanity did not exist as a distinct category, it is not supported by a close scrutiny of the literature. First, eighteenth-century literature was preoccupied with melancholy and madness. Second, many physicians, among them George Cheyne and Richard Blackmore, assumed nervous disorders as their speciality. Kathleen Jones suggests a quite different explanation. She argues that madness came to be seen as a distinct category as a result of an increasingly enlightened and scientific outlook. Andrew Scull castigates this as the 'naive march of progress school'. Although it may be possible to argue on scientific grounds for the treatment of the insane as a distinct category, the empirical evidence for doing this was certainly not available in the nineteenth century. Scientific explanations of insanity were sought after the insane had already been separated from other kinds of deviants. Finally, Foucault argues that until the eigtheenth century madness was a universal presence and that only in the Age of Reason did men feel shame in the presence of the irrational – a shame which the Renaissance had not known. Although in many ways this is a beguiling explanation, particularly when applied to the early eighteenth century and the work of Pope and Swift, it can only be maintained, like Scull's explanation, at a cost of oversimplification and the exclusion of counter evidence. The all-pervasiveness of madness is mostly gathered from Shakespeare's treatment of it. However, a completely contrasting picture of madness can also be gleaned. It is of a fearful and incomprehensible force which is to be kept in subjection by physical brutality (see Chapter 2). Thus the Augustan shame of the irrational is not as novel as Foucault makes out. Nor is it the only set of attitudes to be found in the eighteenth century, or even the most dominating one. Coexisting with the derisory attitudes to the insane found in Pope and Swift are the ideas found in the writings of contemporaneous physicians. Here the attitudes expressed are infinitely patient and serious. The spleen is a widespread and a debilitating affliction which can be controlled, if not entirely cured. The picture which emerges is that of the chronic disability to which one can accommodate, rather than overcome.

The change which occurred at the turn of the century is to be found in the emergence of therapeutic optimism and faith in the possibility of cure, rather than in the development of a distinct category of insanity. Andrew Scull makes the following illuminating point:

> this concern with cure derived, in part at least, from the
> elective affinity of the restorative ideal and of a market system
> which emphasized the notion of a free, rational, self-
> determining individual. One of the major attractions of the
> new discipline of the asylum was that it held out the promise
> of instilling these virtues in that segment of the population
> which departed most radically from them (1974, p.94).

Faith in man's powers of emotional self-discipline and control created a different outlook towards the possibility of a complete cure of nervous disabilities. However, the concomitant of therapeutic optimism was, as Aubrey Lewis points out, a careless treatment of statistics (1955, p.584). One of the chief offenders in this respect was George Man Burrows who claimed a 90 per cent recovery rate for his patients. However, irrespective of actual successes, it is true that attitudes towards insanity underwent a radical change.[1]

Despite the easy and unselfconscious discussion of the spleen and its attendant torments, it is true that those who were socially less well placed experienced vile treatment. From the mid-eighteenth century onwards the revelations of Daniel Defoe and the horrific findings of successive parliamentary committees in the early nineteenth century uncover scenes of astonishing brutality towards the insane. The diet and regular exercise recommended to their prosperous counterparts is reduced to an annual purging and bleeding of all patients in the spring. Yet it seems unlikely that those who cared for the insane considered themselves to be cruel. James Monro, physician to Bethlem, when questioned by a select committee in 1815 about the value of medicine in the treatment of insanity replied:

> With respect to the means used, I really do not depend a vast deal upon medicine; I do not think medicine is the sheet anchor; it is more by management that patients are cured than by medicine; . . . the disease is not cured by medicine, in my opinion. If I am obliged to make that public I must do so (Scull, 1974, p.252).

Asked why he continued to employ purges and bleedings, he replied: 'That has been the practice invariably for years, long before my time; it was handed down to me by my father and I do not know any better practice' (quoted in Scull, ibid., p.252). The conception of the insane as animal-like plus traditional practice combine to render physical force the appropriate method of treatment.

With the reassessment of the nature of insanity comes the possibility of a new method of treatment. Moral management offered the promise of a cure by non-medical means. Pinel saw psychology as a moral science, that is one which concerned itself with the emotions. His treatise was translated into English in 1806 and from that time his ideas were shaped and developed by the English. The first implementation of moral management was to be found at a home for the insane called 'The Retreat' at York. This was founded by the Quaker William Tuke in 1792 for the insane relatives and friends of Quakers. William Tuke was a tea and coffee merchant and the care of the insane was just one of his many philanthropic interests. The principles on which 'The Retreat' was run were later publicized by Samuel Tuke, his grandson, in a book entitled *A Description of the Retreat* (1813). No longer was disease a property of unbridled emotions, but the emotions themselves were the chief weapon in in combating mental disease. He writes:

> If we adopt the opinion that the disease originates in the mind applications made immediately to it, are obviously the most natural; the most likely to be attended with success. If on the

contrary, we conceive that mind is incapable of injury or destruction, and that in all cases of apparent mental derangement, some bodily disease, though unseen and unknown, really exists we shall still readily admit, from the reciprocal action of the two parts of our system upon each other, that the greatest attention is necessary, to whatever is calculated to affect the mind (Tuke, 1813, pp.131-2).

The implication of this view about mental illness is that treatment should appeal to the unimpaired mental faculties. This is, in fact, what Tuke advocates:

Insane persons generally possess a degree of control over their wayward propensities. Their intellectual, active and moral powers, are usually rather perverted and obliterated; and it happens, not infrequently, that one faculty only is affected. The disorder is sometimes still more partial, and can only be detected by erroneous views on one particular subject. On all others the mind appears to retain its wanted correctness (ibid., pp.133-4).

Madness is confined to a limited part of the body and can, therefore, be viewed with a certain detachment by outsiders as well as the patient. Treatment has three components. Tuke writes:

We shall therefore inquire, 1. By what means the power of the patient to control the disorder, is strengthened and assisted. 2. What modes of coercion are employed, when restraint is absolutely necessary. 3. By what means the general comfort of the insane is promoted (ibid., p.133).

Underlying these three principles is an emphasis on the value and power of self-control. By contrast in the eigtheenth century men saw themselves as powerless against and frustrated by madness. Another theme which Tuke singles out for consideration is the use of fear. Whereas fear was one of the principle ways of keeping lunatics in order, this technique is explicitly rejected by Tuke.

The principle of fear which is rarely decreased by insanity, is considered as of great importance in the management of the patients. But it is not allowed to be excited, beyond that degree which naturally arises from the necessary regulations of the family. Neither chains nor corporal punishments are tolerated on any pretext, in this establishment (ibid., p.141).

The patient's better self should be appealed to: 'It is therefore wise to excite as much as possible, the operation of superior motives; and fear ought only to be induced, when a necessary object cannot otherwise be attained.' (ibid., p.143). Fear is rejected on the grounds that it does not work. The treatment of madness does not involve the subjection of a brute force. Rather it involves the gentle persuasion of a wayward or perverted part of the self. Fear is useful neither in the treatment of melancholy nor even of mania:

> If it be true that oppression makes a wise man mad, is it to be supposed that stripes, and insults, and injuries for which the receiver knows no cause, are calculated to make a madman wise? Or would they not exasperate his disease, and excite his resentment? May we not hence most clearly perceive, why furious mania is almost a stranger in the Retreat? (ibid., p.144).

This attitude to fear is in complete contrast with Johnson's view which emphasizes the relief which fear affords the madman.

After the publication of Tuke's book, non-restraint was successfully introduced in a number of asylums including Hanwell in Middlesex and Lincoln Asylum. The two physicians responsible for introducing these changes were John Conolly (1794-1866) and Robert Gardiner Hill (1811-78). During his period as resident medical officer at Lincoln Asylum (1835-1840), Hill achieved the remarkable feat of abolishing all physical restraint, much to the fear and astonishment of medical men and the world at large. Anticipating the fears which this action might have provoked he writes:

> But, it may be demanded, What mode of treatment do you adopt in place of restraint? How do you guard against accidents? How do you provide for the safety of attendants? In short what is the substitute for coercion? The answer may be summed up in a few words, viz – classification – watchfulness – vigilant and unceasing attendance by day and by night – kindness, occupation and attention to health, cleanliness and comfort and the total absence of every description of other occupation by the attendants (Hill, 1839).

Hill specifically denies that medicine has any part to play in the treatment of the insane, unless they are also suffering from physical disease. 'Moral treatment with a view to induce habits of self-control, is all and everything' (ibid., p.45). Given the size of Lincoln Asylum this was no mean achievement.

John Conolly was resident physician at Middlesex County Lunatic Asylum from 1839 to 1844. One of the kindest of men, he described earlier practices with horror and revulsion.

> Indeed it would seem as if, at the period from the middle to near the end of the last century, the superintendents of the insane had become frantic in cruelty, from the impunity with which their despotism was attended. . . . By degrees, restraint became more and more severe, and torture more and more ingenious. Among many cruel devices, an unsuspecting patient was sometimes induced to walk across a treacherous floor; it gave way, and the patient fell into a bath of surprise, and there was half drowned and half frightened to death (Conolly, 1856, p.13).

Conolly goes on to describe patients who were chained to the bottom of a well which was gradually filled with water. Another practice was to tie patients into a gyrating chair first invented by a Dr Cox. The simplest technique of all for subduing patients was to chain them down. Whether such actions were considered cruel by their perpetrators is doubtful. Force was employed because it seemed the only fitting way of subjugating violence. Conolly's description of the gentle reception given to patients under the non-restraint system deserves to be quoted in full:

> But it is part of the non-restraint system to remember, whatever the state and circumstances of a newly admitted patient may be, that he comes to the asylum to be cured, or, if incurable, to be protected and taken care of, and kept out of mischief, and tranquilised; and that the straight-waistcoat effects none of these objects. Therefore, although the patients may arrive so securely fastened as scarcely to be able to move, they are at once released from every ligature and bond and fetter that may have been imposed upon them. They appear themselves surprised at these proceedings; and for a time are tranquil, yet often distrustful, and uncertain in their

movements. Now and then the tranquilising effect of this unexpected liberty is permanent: more frequently it is but temporary. But every newly admitted patient is as soon as possible visited by the medical officers of the asylum. They assure the stranger, by a few kind words, that no ill-treatment is any longer to be feared. This assurance sometimes gains the confidence of the patient at once, and is ever afterward remembered: but in many cases the patient is too much confused to be able to comprehend it. Few or none, however, are quite insensible to the measures immediately adopted in conformity to it.

The wretched clothes are removed; the patient is taken gently to the bathroom and has, probably for the first time, the comfort of a warm bath; which often occasions expressions of remarkable satisfaction. The refreshed patient is taken out of the bath, carefully dried and has clean and comfortable clothing put on: he is then led into the day room, and offered good and well-prepared food. The very plates and knife and fork, and all the simple furniture of the table are cleaner by far than what he has lately been accustomed to, or perhaps such as in his miserable struggling life he never knew before. The non-restraint treatment has commenced and some of its effects already appear.

In short, in an asylum conducted on just principles, and where not only mechanical restraints, but all kinds of neglect and severity are abolished, patients of every rank appreciate and benefit the change. Those who have been well educated express themselves in warm terms of satisfaction, and the poorer classes often convey their simple gratitude in the most affecting terms (Skultans, 1975, pp.150-2).

There is no medical content to this position, rather it is a rediscovery of the humaneness of the insane. The prescriptions for the treatment of the insane embody basic humanitarian values. These represent a revulsion against earlier inhuman attitudes and are undoubtedly permeated by religious values. Finally, 'The Retreat', like some contemporary homes for disturbed children, was run on the model of a family. Patients and staff took meals together and patients were encouraged to work in the house and grounds as soon as they were able to do so. Thus, the most important ingredient of moral management is the restoration of the attributes of humanity to the insane and with it the possibility of encouraging self-control and self-discipline.

The significance of blushing

In this context of self-mastery a curious significance is attributed to blushing – perhaps, because so much weight is attached to moral force and inner effort as a means of counteracting insanity, the outward sign of moral power or conscience is sought. The study of facial expression became a discipline in its own right. Charles Bell (1806), Alexander Morison (1824), Thomas Burgess (1828) and Charles Darwin (1872) all wrote on emotion and its facial expression. Charles Bell summed up the importance and status of this study when he wrote: 'Expression is to passion what language is to thought.' The vogue for studying faces in order to fathom the inner workings of the heart was first introduced by John Caspar Lavater, a Swiss parson whose *Essays on Physiognomy* (1778) became a best seller within a short space of publication. In view of this growing interest in physiognomy it is not surprising that stereotypes of the physiognomy of insanity should emerge.

However, the facial feature to attract most attention is the blush; a whole book is devoted to the subject called *The Physiology or Mechanism of Blushing* (Burgess, 1828). Why did the blush acquire this tremendous meaning? According to Burgess the blush is peculiarly human; animals do not blush. It is the outward and distinctive sign of man's spiritual nature. Burgess argues that unlike other physical expressions of emotion, blushing cannot be caused by physical means. For example, laughter can be caused by tickling and crying by the infliction of physical pain, but the blush only appears when the conscience is moved. Burgess advocates the theological argument that God created the blush

in order that the soul might have sovereign power of displaying in the cheeks the various internal emotions of the moral feelings; so as to serve as a sign to others, that we were violating rules that ought to be held sacred (cited by Darwin, 1872, pp.337-8).

Burgess also distinguishes between the true and the false blush. The false blush is due to a morbid sensibility or over-sensitivity, whereas the true blush emanates from the conscience. He writes:

> After the impression is made on the sensorium which is to excite this phenomenon, we become immediately conscious of what is about to take place, we feel that the will is overpowered – and, for the time being is rendered subordinate to the mental powers, and the emotions of sympathy. Now, from the feeling of our own helplessness, like a bad swimmer when out of his depth, we become flurried, and in our eager attempts to avert the threatened result, by endeavouring to expel from the mind or imagination that association of ideas which is about to bring it forth, we only fix it the more firmly, and ensure its full development to the deep mortification and prostration of our will (1828, p.134).

This connection between blushing, conscience and prostration is particularly interesting and relates to the then current ideas about insanity. Early nineteenth-century theories attached great importance to moral force and the power of the will to fight insanity. One might, therefore, predict that the blush would fit this general configuration. One of the peculiarities of the idiot singled out as of note is his inability to blush, thus portraying his lack of moral sense. The long-standing nineteenth-century debate about whether or not Negroes blush is to be understood against this background. The controversy is not so much a physiological one, as one about moral development. What is at issue, is not a physiological fact, about Negroes, but their moral status as human beings. Whether they are, in fact, fully human. In summary, the inability to blush provides the outward feature of inner failing. Excessive blushing, on the other hand, provides evidence of inner moral failing and often portrays the chronic masturbator.

The importance of the will

Apart from writing specifically describing the practices and institutions of the moral managers, much mid-nineteenth-century medical writing was concerned with describing the strategic role played by the will. A little booklet entitled *Man's Power Over Himself to Prevent or Control Insanity* published anonymously in

1843 but, in fact, written by a Reverend John Barlow is concerned entirely with the benefits derived from an appropriate use of willpower. The following excerpt gives a picture of Barlow's views on insanity:

> The affection of the brain which causes delusions is not madness, but the want of power or resolution to examine them, is. Nothing then but an extent of disease which destroys at once all possibility of reasoning, by annihilating, or entirely changing the structure of the organ, can make a man necessarily mad. In all other cases, the being sane or otherwise, not withstanding considerable disease of brain, depends on the individual himself. He who has given a proper direction to the intellectual force and thus obtained an early command over the bodily organ by habituating it to processes of calm reasoning, remains sane amid all the vagaries of sense; while he who has been the slave rather than the master of his animal nature, listens to its dictates without question even when distorted by disease, – and is mad. A fearful result of an uncultivated childhood, or of a manhood too much devoted to the active, money getting employments of this world, which so often form the chief pursuit of life. These, instead of strengthening the mind to bear the reverses of fortune which all are liable to, but render it more acutely sensible of the disappointments incident to such pursuits, and form too often one of the proximate causes of this terrible affliction.

> If I am right in what I have advanced, a man may labour under a mental delusion, and yet be a responsible agent: and if sanity or insanity be in a great many instances the consequences of a greater or less resolution in exerting the power of reasoning still possessed, the same kind of motives which influence a man in common life, are still available, though they may require to be somewhat heightened (ibid., pp.27-8).

A decade later Daniel Noble in his *Elements of Psychological Medicine* (1853) writes of the importance of energetically exercising the will.

> I would say a word concerning the importance of energetically exercising the will, in resistance to unwanted ideas that present

themselves so often to a morbid fancy, when disorder of the digestive organs depresses the emotional sensibility. If this were well understood and acted-upon, there is no doubt that many cases of melancholia and emotional delusion would be prevented. I have at this time a gentleman who frequently suffers from nervous dispepsia, and who during his attacks is decidedly hypochondriacal. He tells me that on these occasions, ideas the most outrageous and bizarre will generally haunt his disordered imagination; that, for example, the notion of cutting off the nose of one of his servants is particularly vivid. There is not in this gentleman's family the slightest tendency to insanity, as far as I can learn; and he himself a strong-minded man, with a firm and resolute will; and moreover, he thoroughly appreciates the actual circumstances of his own case. He has often told me that, but for strong volitional efforts, he believes he would have been insane (Noble, 1853, pp.334-5).

The power of the individual to combat insanity is a new and optimistic theme which emerges in the nineteenth century. It must be set against a wider background of social and geographical mobility, optimism in the powers of the individual to make his own way and overcome adverse circumstances and a mood of romanticism which turns inwards to examine the emotional and intellectual resources of the individual.

Moral insanity

During the period of moral management a new diagnosis is made – moral insanity. The term moral insanity was first used by James Cowles Prichard, the Bristol ethnologist and physician. Prichard defined the term as follows: 'This form of mental disease . . . consists of a morbid perversion of the feelings, affections, habits, without any hallucination or erroneous conviction impressed upon the understanding; it sometimes coexists with an apparently unimpaired state of the intellectual faculties' (1833, p.14). Madness is located in inappropriate emotions and feelings rather than in defective reasoning. This view contrasts completely with Locke's view of madness as a self-contained defect of reasoning. Rather Prichard's ideas stem from the early eighteenth-century tradition in which unbridled passions are thought dangerous and feared. A forerunner of this tradition is Hobbes's account of the madman:

> that madness is nothing else, but too much appearing passion, may be gathered out of the effects of wine, which are the same with those of the evil disposition of the organs. For the variety of behaviour in men that have drunk too much, is the same with that of madmen: some of them raging, others laughing, all extravagantly, but according to their several domineering passions, for the effect of the wine does but remove dissimulation, and take from them the sight of the deformity of their passions. For I believe that most sober men, when they walk alone without care and employment of the mind would be unwilling that the vanity and extravagance of their thoughts should be publicly seen; which is a confession that passions unguided, are for the most part mere madness (Hobbes, 1962, p.107).

Moral insanity is the final outcome of 'passions unguided'. Attention has shifted from 'lesions of the understanding' to perversions of feeling. Prichard specifically argues that Locke's account is 'far too limited an account of madness' (Skultans, 1975, p.180). And he goes on to cite

> cases of a different description, in which the intellectual faculties appear to have sustained but little injury, while the feelings and affections, the moral and active principles of the mind are strangely perverted, the power of self-government is lost or greatly impaired; and the individual is found to be incapable, not of talking or reasoning upon any subject proposed to him, for this he will often do with great shrewdness and volubility, but of conducting himself with decency and propriety in the business of life. His wishes and inclinations, his attachments, his likings and dislikings have all undergone a morbid change, and this change appears to be the originating cause, or to lie at the foundation of any disturbance which the understanding itself may have sustained, and even in some instances to form throughout the chief character or constituent feature of the disease (ibid., p.181).

One of the difficulties which this variety of insanity presents is distinguishing between it and mere eccentricity. Prichard writes:

> There are many individuals living at large and not entirely
> separated from society, who are affected, in a certain degree,
> with this modification of insanity. They are reputed persons of
> a singular, wayward, and eccentric character. An attentive
> observer will often recognise something remarkable in their
> manners and habits, which may lead him to entertain doubts
> as to their entire sanity, and circumstances are sometimes
> discovered on inquiry, which add strength to this suspicion
> (ibid., pp.185-6).

However, the differences between mere eccentricity and moral
insanity are left imprecise. The cases which Prichard cites suggest
that his term morally insane did not merely refer to people whose
behaviour was anti-social, but who felt inappropriate or degenerate
emotions. Prichard gives the following case study to illustrate the
history of moral insanity:

> J.K.–, a farmer, several of whose relatives had been the
> subjects of mental derangement, was a man of sober and
> domestic habits, and frugal and steady in his conduct, until
> about his 45th year, when his disposition appeared to have
> become suddenly changed in a manner which excited the
> surprise of his friends and neighbours and occasioned grief and
> vexation in his family. He became wild, excitable, thoughtless,
> full of schemes and absurd projects. He would set out and
> make long journeys into distant parts of the country to
> purchase cattle and farming stock, of which he had no means
> of disposing; he brought a number of carriages, hired an
> expensive house ready furnished, which had been inhabited by a
> person much above his rank, and was unsuitable to his
> condition: he was irascible and impetuous, quarrelled with his
> neighbours, and committed an assault upon the clergyman of
> the parish, for which he was indicted and bound to take his
> trial. At length his wife became convinced that he was mad
> and made application for his confinement in a lunatic asylum,
> which was consequently effected. The medical practitioners
> who examined him were convinced of his insanity by
> comparing his late wild habits and unaccountable conduct with
> the former tenor of his life, taking into consideration the

tendency to disease which was known to prevail in his family. The change in his character alone had produced a full conviction of his madness in his friends and relatives. When questioned as to the motives which had induced him to some of his late proceedings, he gave clear plausible reason for almost every part of his conduct. After a time passed in great seclusion, his mind became gradually tranquillised, the morbid excitement of his temper and feelings disappeared; he was set at liberty, and has since conducted himself with propriety (ibid., p.184).

Although there are elements of anti-social behaviour in this description it is clearly not psychopathic. The emphasis is on its inappropriateness and the unpredictability of moods. What we would term psychopathic behaviour was described in detail and with relish by Henry Maudsley in his accounts of the morally degenerate (see Chapter 8).

Note

[1] Attitudes to moral management and its powers of cure appear to have come full circle. At first the new approach was welcomed with enthusiasm and promised a near 100 per cent cure rate, only to be subsequently discarded as ineffective in treating the large numbers of incurables. However, this pattern is not unique to moral management but is common to all new forms of psychiatric treatment and, indeed, medical treatment. The destiny of various psychiatric therapies is documented in a particularly interesting article by Garfield Tourney.

> As one views the development of psychiatric therapies since the time of Pinel, one is impressed by the life cycle of new treatment methods; the initial enthusiasm and the report of remarkable results are tempered by the application of a more critical study and evaluation and resulting in less impressive statistics. Finally, the method is accepted with many limitations or rejected as being of questionable or negligible value. Initial statistics often indicate results of 90% recovery or marked improvement, but in subsequent studies these figures are reduced to 50-60% in the psychoneuroses and 30-40% in schizophrenia (Tourney, 1967, p.785).

Tourney attributes the decreased success rates to increasing scepticism and scientific rigour. However, it may well be that, as in the case of moral management, other social and economic factors enter and, therefore, affect the figures for cure.

5
Masturbational insanity

During the early nineteenth century masturbation became interesting to medicine. Medicine gained two new diagnostic categories: spermatorrhoea, or excessive loss of sperm, and masturbational insanity. Both convey anxiety about loss of semen. The history of interest in this area is worth considering and requires some explanation. Why did masturbation come to be thought of as an activity of general importance, let alone of medical importance? Why did this happen in the mid-nineteenth century?

Literature contains few references to masturbation. John Aubrey is unusual in describing the young Duke of Buckingham's solitary pursuits.

> Mr. Hobbes told me, that G. Duke of Buckingham had at
> Paris when he was about twenty years old, desired him to read
> Geometric to him: his Grace had great natural parts, and
> quickness of wit; Mr. Hobbes read, and his Grace did not
> apprehend, which Mr. Hobbes wondered at: at last Mr.
> Hobbes observed that his Grace was at mastrupation (his hand
> in his codpiece). This is a very improper age, for that reason
> for learning . . . (Aubrey, 1950).

Otherwise one has to wait until the twentieth century before it becomes an acceptable literary theme. 'Scientific' interest in the subject can be given a precise date of origin. In 1710 an anonymous clergyman published a treatise on masturbation entitled *Onania, or the Heinous Sin of Self-Pollution.* Very many editions appeared in the course of the century. *Onania* is written with elegance and style. This terseness of style seems typical of eighteenth-century writing and was lost by later nineteenth-century physicians. The flavour of the book may be caught by quoting the opening sentence:

> Self-pollution is that unnatural practice by which persons of either sex may defile their own bodies without the assistance of others, whilst yielding to filthy imaginations they endeavour to imitate and procure to themselves, that sensation which God has ordained to attend the carnal commerce of the two sexes, for the continuance of our species (anon., 1710, p.1).

The first edition is just under 100 pages long. Later editions are slightly longer and include a correspondence between the author and a critic of the book. The debate concerns the relative sinfulness of fornication and masturbation. The critic argues that self-pollution is the lesser of two evils since it avoids the debauchment of innocent women. The argument is rather similar to St Thomas's deprecation of incest. He argues that incest is doubly sinful since it compounds feelings of familial love with those of physical love. *Onania* was in many ways ahead of its time, in that it appears neither to have reflected current concerns and anxieties nor to have influenced them. An easier more relaxed attitude to sexual activity was the prevailing norm. Burton provides a good illustration of this. He writes with feeling of the tortures of unappeased sexual desire and the uncharitable attitude of neighbours:

> They will by all means quench their neighbour's house, if it be
> on fire; but that fire of lust which breaks out into such
> lamentable flames they will not take notice of; their own
> bowels often times flesh and blood, shall so rage and burn; and
> they shall not see it (Burton, 1621, p.304).

In England these ideas acquired their greatest popularity in the mid-nineteenth century. During the 1840s and 1850s there is a spate of books dealing with loss of semen. The work of Ellis (1838), Dawson (1840), Lallemand in English translation (1847), Milton (1854), Curling (1856) and Acton (1865) all deal with this subject and appeared within a few years of each other.

Masturbation, or, 'the primal addiction' as Freud was later to call it, is one focus of anxiety. Another more general and basic area of concern is seminal loss, which may, but need not, be caused by masturbation. A generally accepted, if not clear, definition of spermatorrhoea is given by Curling in his book *A Practical Treatise on the Diseases of the Testis*:

The emissions may, however, be more frequent than is consistent with health, and too readily excited, so much so, indeed, as to affect virility, and to give rise to constitutional symptoms of a serious character. These excessive spermatic discharges constitute the complaint termed spermatorrhoea (1856, p.386).

This loss may be voluntary as in intercourse and masturbation, or involuntary as in 'nocturnal pollutions' or other emissions, for example, whilst at stool. Typically, the picture presented is that of a dribbling penis. Throughout the 1840s and 1850s, physicians showed increasing concern that insufficient attention was paid to the dangers of seminal loss. For example:

It has always appeared strange to me that this affection should remain abandoned by the profession to a few solitary specialists, and for the benefit of the vile harpies who prey on this class of victims. Surgery which has wrested so much from empiricism and ignorance, seems disposed to yield up this, as if it were, debateable land, to chance, philosophy, utter neglect or quackery (Milton, 1854, p.243).

Lallemand, the French specialist on spermatorrhoea, describes it as: 'A disease that degrades man, poisons the happiness of his best days, and ravages society' (1847, p.ii).

In part, these fears reflect uneasiness about sexuality as such. For example, Milton, in advising on the treatment and prevention of spermatorrhoea, reveals a general squeamishness on the subject: 'Over and over again a patient has noticed that getting up betimes, as soon as he awoke in fact, avoided that which a longer stay in that bundle of paradoxes, the bed, would have induced' (1887, p.170). However, a general coyness about sexuality does not explain the particular interest in seminal loss. Seminal loss in intercourse is set apart as being rather less harmful. Spitzka, for example, writes: '. . . there is a discrepancy between the results of natural and artificial excesses' (1887, p.225). And later he says of natural sexual excess that it has 'none of the perversions or emotional anomalies so characteristic of the latter. . . . Nature has so arranged that there are limits to sexual excess. . . . No such limits check the onanist' (ibid., 225). However, it is precisely the loss of semen involved in sexual intercourse, rather than the activity itself, which is considered pernicious. For this reason male masturbation is singled out for consideration. Spitzka writes: 'The effects of such indulgence are less serious in the female owing to the less exhausting nature of the discharges.'

In fact, beliefs about seminal loss constitute a distinct syndrome. Most writers on the subject are agreed on the causes of spermatorrhoea. These include constipation, worms, piles, gonorrhoea, heat, heavy bedclothes, highly seasoned food, alcohol, intense application of the mind and excessive indulgence in sexual intercourse, usually of a promiscuous kind. The effects of spermatorrhoea are similar to those of masturbation. In general these are debilitating. In particular, there is an intimate connection between seminal loss and the condition of the brain. There is an inability to sustain mental and bodily fatigue; a heaviness in the head; giddiness; sleeplessness. Interestingly, the appetite increases, often becoming voracious. Dawson writes: 'I have generally found unnatural seminal discharge accompanied with increased appetite, owing to the necessity which the system feels, of compensating the daily losses which it sustains' (1840, p.6). Long-term effects, like those of masturbation, are more serious: parched skin, loss of hair, stammering, deafness, blindness, form part of the familiar list.

Masturbation forms a sub-category of the interest in loss of semen. The picture of the typical masturbator is one of extreme selfishness. Spitzka described a patient representing this category as follows:

> His demeanour was obtrusive, mean and selfish. He sat out all my other patients on the morning he called, withdrew to the waiting-room, under indignant protests, when I represented to him that I could not keep a physician accompanying patients, who had come a great distance, waiting any longer, he having already consumed two hours. He came in repeatedly, and finally, after I had finished, he took possession of the field, and as I hurried off to my much delayed lunch, he exclaimed: 'Hurry up, doctor, do not be long; I have a great deal to tell you yet. My case is of more importance than any other you ever had; I am the most important man in my family' (1887, p.239).

Maudsley describes the consequences of masturbation begun early in life as follows: 'we have degenerate beings produced who as regards moral character are very much what eunuchs are represented to be – cunning, deceitful, liars, selfish, in fact, morally insane; while their physical and intellectual vigour is further damaged by the exhausting vice' (1868, p.156).

Another characteristic of the chronic masturbator is his shyness, his timidity, and, in particular, his inability to look others in the eye. Allnatt describes a patient of his who 'entered the room with a timid and suspicious air, and appeared to quail like an irresolute maniac when the eye was fixed irresolutely upon him' (1843, p.654). David Skae, the Scottish physician who first identified a particular brand of insanity which he termed masturbatory, also singles out similar features of the masturbator:

> that vice produces a group of symptoms which are quite characteristic, and easily recognized, and give to the cases a special natural history. The peculiar imbecility and shy habits of the very youthful victim, the suspicion and fear, and dread, and suicidal impulses, the palpitations and scared look, and feeble body of the older offenders, passing gradually into dementia or fatuity, with other characteristic features familiar to all of you, which I do not stop to enlarge on, all combine to stamp this as a natural order or family (Skae, 1863, p.315).

The sad psychological portrait of the masturbator is reinforced by the physical appearance of sallow complexion and dark ringed eyes. However, masturbation is not only one among the ingredients of a character type, it is also the cause of further disabilities. General weakness is a most common result, followed by headache, backache, acne, indigestion, blindness, deafness, epilepsy and, finally, death. In fact, the syndrome produced is very similar to that of spermatorrhoea. Lastly, an inability to participate in social life develops.

Although interest in masturbation persists into the latter part of the nineteenth century, there is a reinterpretation of its nature. Maudsley, for example, in his early paper on masturbation in the *Journal of Mental Science* (1868) regards the activity with the abhorrence due to a form of moral degeneracy. It is worth quoting one of Maudsley's cases at length.

> As an example of the high-pitched and absurd sentiments professed sometimes by these degraded beings, I may mention the case of a gentleman who had a plan for curing the social evil. He set forth with great feeling and energy the miserable

and wicked thing which it was that many of the most beautiful
women should be degraded to satisfy the worst lusts of men;
and professed himself to be grievously distressed by the sin and
evil which were caused thereby. How were so much vice and
misery to be done away with? His plan, which he practised
himself and proposed that others should follow was to
masturbate every morning into a tumbler of water and to drink
it. He argued that the lust was thus satisfied without injury to
any other person, whilst the man himself was strengthened by
the nourishment afforded to his brain. Here, then, as in other
cases, was a mind enervated by vicious practices, dwelling
continually on sexual subjects, and concocting, not designedly,
but with unconscious hypocrisy, an excuse for the vice which
wrecked his life. It is a curious thing that to such a state of
moral degradation have patients of this class come, that they
will actually defend their vice on some pretence or other
(Maudsley, 1868, p.160).

One is reminded of the earlier debate in *Onania,* although this time
one cannot help but admire the rigour and consistency of this
patient's logic. When Maudsley comes to reconsider the subject in
The Pathology of Mind (1879) he sees masturbation as a product of
bad inheritance over which the patient has little control. In line with
this reappraisal is the increasing insistence on preventive surgical
measures in contrast to the earlier moral exhortations.

At first sight the mid-nineteenth-century interest in
spermatorrhoea and masturbation seems incompatible with the
concurrent commitment to moral management. Medical interest in
the dire consequences of masturbation may appear to twentieth-
century readers as an unwarranted and violent intrusion into privacy
and as such contrasts with the kind treatment of patients by the moral
managers. The 1840s and 1850s are also the period during which the
major works of the moral managers appear. The moral managers
urged the abandonment of physical restraint which had been central
to eighteenth-century therapeutic practice. Instead, they advocated
psychological techniques. Appeal to the conscience and will of the
patient was suggested. In this way, it was thought, the power of self-
control could be nurtured and the art of self-government furthered.
However, both areas of interest presuppose self-control and thus
complement each other. Both must be seen as an expression of

concern with continence in its widest sense. Disapproval of venery is but another aspect of the pursuit of moderation and discipline. Masturbation, one of the most solitary of activities, is regarded as the arch-vice precisely because of the hopes vested in the individual. In typifying loss of control, it is seen as the moral failure *par excellence*. Foucault, of course, would see medical interest in masturbation as further evidence of his thesis that moral management represents total control of the patient or madness mastered.

These ideas cannot be explained, as Szasz tries to do, as an attempt by the medical profession to control human sexuality (1971). Neither can 'the masturbatory hypothesis' be seen as a fallacy of reasoning, as Hare would like it, which is dispelled by the increasing clarity and coherence of medical thought (1962). Nor can it be explained as a product of the emotional immaturity and prurience of the physicians, as Comfort claims (1967). One of the most illuminating works against which to set the masturbatory hypothesis is J. A. Banks's *Prosperity and Parenthood* (1954). As the title suggests, Banks examines the relationship between the postponement of marriage and expectations as to what constitutes an appropriate middle-class life style. According to Banks such ideas appear from the 1830s onwards. 'A "proper" time to marry! – more and more as the century wore on this became the theme of the middle classes, until the words "prudence" and "postponement" became the two most hackneyed in their vocabulary' (ibid., p.36). The situation is even more graphically described in an editorial taken from *The Times*:

> The laws which society imposes in the present day in respect of young men belonging to the middle class are, in the highest degree, unnatural, and are the real cause of our social corruptions. The father of a family has in many instances, risen from a comparatively humble origin to a position of easy competence. His wife has her carriage; he associates with men of wealth greater than his own. His sons reach the age when in the natural course of things they ought to marry and establish a home for themselves. It would seem no great hardship that a young couple should begin on the same level as their parents began, and be content for the first few years with the bare necessaries of life, and there are thousands who, were it not for society, would gladly marry on such terms. But here the tyrant world interposes; the son must not marry until he can maintain

on much the same footing as his father's (*The Times,* 7 May, 1857).

Late marriages may, in part, be responsible for the growth of anxiety about masturbation. However, beliefs about masturbation and the masturbator must also be set against beliefs about the nature of man and the growing role attributed to the will. Although, or perhaps because, beliefs about will-power deal with such an elusive and intangible area of human nature they give rise to certain crude bodily stereotypes. The blush provides the outward evidence of a finely tuned moral sensibility. Similarly, the chronic masturbator embodies the antithesis of all the valued characteristics of the period. He is the polar opposite of nature's gentleman: the person who can get by on the strength of inner resourcefulness and outer accomplishments. He provides the prototype of uncontrolled and undisciplined behaviour.

6
Femininity and illness

The psychic vulnerability of women provides an unbroken thread in the medical literature. An historical study such as this shows that beliefs about feminine nature are relatively unchanging. For this reason it is not easy to relate beliefs about feminine nature to social and historical changes.

The admission figures to lunatic asylums tell us little. There are no figures for admissions to asylums before 1844. Thereafter there is a slight preponderance of women and the ratio of male to female patients is roughly 4:5. The preponderance of women is more marked in the pauper lunatic population (see Table 2). In workhouses there are a third more lunatic women than men. However, these figures do not explain the exaggerated ideas about female vulnerability, ideas which are not reflected in the lunacy figures since many female complaints could be dealt with at home. Hysteria was, by definition, a feminine complaint and also a domestic one. It could and often was dealt with at home with the help of visits from the family physician. Thus one important feminine complaint would not figure in the lunacy figures.

An important parallel theme to the history of ideas about female vulnerability is the history of the double standard. Keith Thomas describes this idea as follows: 'Stated simply, it is the view that unchastity in the sense of sexual relations before or outside marriage, if an offence, is none the less a mild and pardonable one, but for a woman a matter of the utmost gravity' (1959, p.195). The double standard rests on another assumption, namely 'the view that men have property in women and that the value of this property is immeasurably diminished if the woman at any time has sexual relations with anyone other than her husband' (ibid., p.210). Thus the double standard depends on women's position relative to men. Furthermore, 'the value set on female chastity varied directly according to the extent to which it was considered that women's function was a purely sexual one' (ibid., p.213). The ultimate glorification of female sexuality was to be found in the desexualization of women embodied in the eighteenth-century heroine Pamela – 'delicate, insipid, fainting at the first sexual advance and utterly devoid of feelings towards her admirer until the marriage knot was tied' (ibid., p.215). The persistence of the double standard with only minor variations over time indicates that the basic characteristics of women's position in society have remained unchanged. Throughout the period under consideration men have property in women and women are men's legal and financial dependants. This position accounts not only for the persistence of the double standard, but also for women's alleged proneness to nervous disorders. Their dependence on men is reflected in their child-like affectability. Women remained to a greater or lesser extent subordinate to men and were thought to be more prone to nervous and emotional complaints. As early as 1683 Thomas Tryon was aware of the greater vulnerability of women particularly in relation to alcohol:

> for it is not only against feminine nature to drink strong
> drinks, but also destructive to the generation of mankind; it
> makes them masculine and robustick, filling them with fury
> and madness and many other indecencies . . . The nature of
> women will not bear excess in meat and drinks, as men will
> without manifest danger to their healths, and also to the
> healths of their children; most windy deseases in both women
> and children, being caused by their intemperance both in
> quantity and quality (ibid., p.10).

If feminine nature itself does not protect women against excess, then they are that much more at its mercy.

This constitutional proneness needs to be carefully examined. Although it has always been mentioned in the medical literature, it was most written about in the nineteenth century. John Haslam, the Apothecary to Bethlem wrote: 'In females who become insane the desease is often connected with the peculiarities of their sex' (1817, p.4). The 'peculiarities' he alluded to are of two kinds: emotional and reproductive. The emotional vulnerability puts women on a par with children. This view is succinctly and explicitly put by Thomas Laycock, author of *A Treatise on Nervous Diseases of Women* (1840): 'It is widely acknowledged that the affectability of the female sex has its counterpart in that of children' (ibid., p.131). Their labileness and affectability not only increases their proneness to illness but also decreases the benefits which they are likely to reap from education. One nineteenth-century writer on nervous diseases describes education for women as 'mental persecution' and women as its 'victims'. This is a situation which 'daringly isolates those natural laws of organization, which have fated the cerebral structures of woman, less qualified for those severe ordeals, than those of her brother man' (Maddock, 1854, p.17). In the late nineteenth century the debate about women and education intensified, as a result of the increasing articulateness of women's demands for education. The other source of constitutional unfitness relates to the constraints imposed upon women by virtue of their sexual and reproductive role. These two sources of vulnerability are referred to time and again by many writers.

Views about female insanity are coloured by the prevailing views about women. Burton, a bachelor, and a life-long sufferer from melancholy and author of *The Anatomy of Melancholy,* although not entirely misogynist is certainly ambivalent about feminine assets. He writes:

> That other madness is a woman. . . . Pleasant at first she is, that fair plant to the eye, but poison to the taste, the rest as bitter as wormwood in the end, and sharp as a two-edged sword. Her house is the way to hell, and goes down to the chambers of death.

Burton is equally sceptical about women's last refuge – tears. His phrase is as scathing as it is memorable. 'You may as well be sorry for a woman crying as for a goose because it is barefoot.' However, the alternatives are not enticing to Burton. He is too painfully aware of the torments of unconsummated passion. In view of the possible perils his sage and sober counsel is marriage. 'Tis a hazard both ways I confess, to live single or to marry . . . God sent us all good wives, every man his wish in this kind, and me mine' (ibid., p.624). However, the blessings afforded by womankind are mixed and Burton is cautious in advocating marriage as the lesser of two evils.

The melancholy which Burton ascribes to women is related to 'those vicious vapours which come from menstruous blood'. Furthermore, there is a 'fulginous exhalation of corrupt seed, troubling the brain, heart and mind. . . . The whole malady proceeds from that inflammation, putricity, black smoky vapours, etc., from thence comes care, sorrow and anxiety, obfuscation of spirits, agony, desperation, and the like' (ibid., p.272). The symptoms to which these exhalations of corrupt seed give rise are many and varied.

> a brutish kind of dotage, troublesome sleep, terrible dreams in the night, a foolish kind of bashfulness to some, perverse conceits and opinions, dejection of mind, much discontent, preposterous judgement. They are apt to loathe, dislike, disdain, to be weary of every object, etc., each thing almost is tedious to them, they pine away, void of counsel, apt to weep, and tremble, timorous, fearful, sad, and out of all hope of better fortunes (ibid., pp.272-3).

Their sources of discomfort are moreover constantly changing:

> now their brests, now their hypochrondries, belly and sides, then their heart and head aches, now heat, then wind, now this, now that offends, they are weary of all; and yet will not, cannot again tell how, where or what offends them though they be in great pain and agony, and frequently complain, grieving, sighing, weeping, and discontented still, *sine causa manifesta* (ibid., p.302).

The best remedy for these very varied and distressing ills is 'to see them well placed, and married to good husbands in due time'. Alternatively, religion, work and a disciplined life are the remedies which cure most feminine ills. For this reason Burton argues that:

> Tis seldom shall you see an hired servant, a poor handmaid, though ancient, that is kept hard to her work, and bodily labour; a coarse country wench troubled in this kind, but noble virgins, nice gentlewomen, such as are solitary and idle, live at ease, lead a life out of action and employment, that fare well, in great houses and jovial companies . . . subject to passions such for the most part are misaffected and prone to this disease (ibid., p.273).

Symptomatology, epidemiology and cure are presented in one fell swoop in a section three-and-a-half pages long; in a book over 700 pages long that is quite a feat of brevity. What it does show is Burton's stereotype of woman and her ailments: woman is undisciplined and her ailments stem from this lack of regulation and the hazards associated with her sexuality.

The contrast is striking between women's melancholy and the contemporaneous affliction *The Elizabethan Malady*. Melancholy, when it affects women, is always described as women's melancholy. It is not described in the attractive terms of other kinds of melancholy. The epidemics of melancholy which swept through the fashionable circle of London from 1580 onwards curiously bypassed women. Lawrence Babb writes: 'For some time melancholy men were so numerous in London that they constituted a social type, often called the *Malcontent* (1959, p.3). Elizabethan ideas followed the Aristotelian tradition which associates melancholy with poetic inspiration and wit. Robert Burton is following this tradition when he describes melancholy men as 'of a deep reach, excellent apprehension, judicious, wise and witty' (1621, p.451). Women's ailments are, needless to say, never characterized as the Aristotelian variety of melancholy – that category is reserved for men.

By the late seventeenth century a flourishing misogynist literature was circulating. Interestingly, it is during this period that hysteria appears as a significant diagnosis in the literature. There are many misogynous books, among them Edward Ward's *Female Policy Detected, or the Arts of the Designing Woman Laid Open* (1704). It seems to have been written from personal and painful experience in its distrust of women and in its representation of them as manipulative and scheming it is representative of much literature of the period.

> Love a woman with moderation that loves you to excess; her
> passion will naturally reduce itself to the same equality, for no
> extremes are lasting, and then you have the advantage, for the
> continuance of a little love shows a constant temper, and looks
> friendly and obliging, when a passion cooled to the same
> indifferency will look slighting and neglective; besides he that
> loves a woman too much, is apt to love himself too little (ibid.,
> p.12).

A more moving testimony of personal suffering is found in the

following lines: 'Is not the bee hived for his honey, the sheep sheared
for his fleece . . . But what labour or cost thou bestowest on a woman
is cast away, for she will yield thee no profit at all' (ibid., p.74). This
flourishing of misogynous literature can be understood by looking at
changing marriage patterns. A historian writes of the increasing
material considerations to which marriage and personal sentiment
were subordinated in the eighteenth as opposed to the sixteenth and
seventeenth centuries:

> Calculations of material interest have played an important part
> in marriage, between propertied families in almost all periods.
> But there is evidence that in the early eighteenth century they
> were more important than for the early seventeenth and
> sixteenth century and that the material interests were once
> exclusively a matter of wealth (K. J. Habakkuk, 1950, p.24).

Thus increasingly marriage was subordinated to wealth. This was due
to the greater difficulty in acquiring husbands and the increasing cost
of marrying off daughters. (The size of portions or dowries increased
during the seventeenth century.)

> The increase in portions does therefore indicate a change in the
> terms of marriage settlements in favour of the husbands. Why
> did this happen?
> Contemporaries were apt to attribute the rising scale of
> portions to the greater competition in the marriage market of
> the daughters, especially the heiresses of merchant families
> (ibid., p.23).

And the competition arose because of a fall in the number of eligible
men due to losses sustained during the Civil War and the wars against
Louis XIV. This argument correlating marriage patterns with
stereotypes about feminine nature is essentially demographic and has
been thoroughly explored by Roger Thompson in his book *Women
in Stuart England and America* (1974). Thompson argues that the
value placed upon women varies inversely with their scarcity. Thus in
America during the seventeenth century, where men far
outnumbered women, women enjoyed high status and considerable
freedom. Whereas in England during the same period there was an
excess of females over males. Demographic imbalance and
difficulties within marriage were reflected by what another historian
Keith Thomas in his history of the double standard describes as 'the

extreme wenching attitude' (1959, p.195). The females of Sheridan's plays, for example, are shown to have been such for real reasons. (Demographic imbalance or, at least, a belief in demographic imbalance was to make an equally important contribution to women's ill health in the mid-nineteenth century.)

During this period of ambivalence towards women the number of feminine complaints increased. Thomas Sydenham developed a new insight into the definition and treatment of hysteria:

> Of all the chronic diseases hysteria – unless I err – is the commonest; since just as fevers – taken with their accompaniments – equal two thirds of the number of all chronic diseases taken together, so do hysterical complaints (or complaints so called) take one half of the remaining third. As to females if we except those who lead a hard life, there is hardly one is wholly free from them – and females, be it remembered form one half of the adults of the world (Sydenham, 1848, vol. 2, p.54).

Medical interest in hysteria dates from Edward Jorden's publication of *A Briefe Discourse of a Disease called Suffocation of the Mother* (1603). The book was written as a result of Jorden's involvement in the trial of Elizabeth Jackson who was accused of bewitching fourteen-year-old Mary Glover. Jorden was among the four doctors who examined Mary Glover and his diagnosis was one of hysteria rather than sorcery. Jorden argued that paralysis and convulsions were symptoms of disease rather than signs of sorcery. The account which he gives of hysteria is essentially the ancient uterine theory in which suppression of menstruation and sexual abstinence play a major part in the development of disease. However, he describes the human predicament in graphic terms, 'the perturbations of the mind' also play a significant role: 'For seeing we are not masters of our own affections, we are like battered cities, without walls, a ship tossed in the sea, exposed to all manner of assaults and dangers, even to the overthrow of our own bodies.'

William Harvey was also interested in gynaecological and hysterical disorders and like others took over ancient uterine theories of hysteria: 'No one of the least experience can be ignorant what grievous symptoms arise when the uterus either rises up or falls down, or is in any way put out of place, or is seized with spasm.' His aetiological explanations too are traditional: 'How many incurable diseases are also brought about by unhealthy menstrual discharges or from over-abstinence from sexual intercourse when the passions are strong.' By contrast Thomas Willis the seventeenth-century neurologist was emphatic in denying the uterine origin of hysteria. He argued 'that the distemper named from the womb is chiefly and primarily convulsive and chiefly depends on the brain and the nervous stock (system) being affected' (Willis, 1664). Being a more consistent empiricist than Harvey, Willis advanced anatomical evidence to refute the uterine theory: 'The womb is of so small bulk in virgins and widows and is so strictly tied by neighbouring parts, that it cannot of itself be moved or ascend from its place.' And he offered further evidence that hysteria lies within the head by referring to the findings of post-mortem examinations.

These accounts of hysteria draw on a fund of established ideas about the disease. For example, it is interesting that despite his nosological sophistication Sydenham reinstated the uterine theory of hysteria. Similarly, although Harvey had an empirical approach in other areas, he did not when it came to hysteria. Since hysteria was thought to produce an accumulation of putrid humours, one of the forms of treatment involved purification of the blood by purging and bleeding. Subsequent fortification of the blood was achieved by taking iron filings and horse-back riding.

The medical literature of the seventeenth and eighteenth centuries has many accounts of hysteria. To what extent is this medical preoccupation reflected in the literature of the period? At this point the weeping heroine makes her appearance in literature, and in a context where the main theme of the novel is, according to Christopher Hill, to 'examine the effect on men and women of property marriage and all that goes with it' (Hill, 1968, p.357). He notes that 'a wife who broke her marriage vows is more criminal than a husband who did the same because of the doubts that would be cast on the succession of property' (ibid., p.367). Dr Johnson summarized the situation by describing the chastity of women as 'of the utmost importance as all property depends upon it'. Heroines are 'pretty uniformly called upon to register sensibility by tears' (Needham and Utter, 1937, p.96). Fiction becomes a veritable quagmire. Why do tears come to dominate fiction at this particular period? One answer is suggested by Needham and Utter:

> Why does the period known in the history of thought as the
> Age of Reason record itself in the history of the novel in terms

of tearful hysteria that would disgrace a girls' boarding school? Two answers suggest themselves perhaps because it was the Age of Reason. The age cannot be completely one of reason so long as emotion, which it cannot suppress or destroy, remains outside its control. Since it cannot eradicate emotion it must govern it by rules. There shall be no emotion save such as is decorous in the drawing-room . . . (ibid., p.102).

Second, the melancholic outlook is an indication of social aspiration. The 'melancholy posture' implies suppression of feeling, and is opposite to peasant insensibility and peasant noisiness of expression. Tears reflect increasing social differentiation. According to Needham and Utter 'Liquid sorrow has babbled through the runways of literature since its earliest stages, but tears show little social significance before Feudalism' (ibid., p.105). And later in history this elaboration of feeling is transmitted to the novel.

It is this romance tradition of aristocratic feeling which passes at long last into the novel. The romance of feudal times directly or indirectly sets up a sort of code for the use and expression of the emotions of ladies and gentlemen. Ladies may weep on all occasions of vexation, pain and sorrow. Gentlemen may weep for the pains of love, in sympathy with others, especially as a mark of chivalric friendship, and in sorrow for the death of others. They seem to show stoicism on the endurance of physical pain, particularly in combat or battle, and in the endurance of the pangs of death (ibid., p.106).

The grand heroine of eighteenth-century fiction, Pamela, is well versed in the art of weeping:

Pamela, working girl though she is, moves in the fashionable world. Since she is to be promoted to membership in it, Richardson has her in training from the start, and though she 'knows her place', ladylike sensibility always fits her as closely as her piety. She weeps for good cause at various times when her master is badgering her (ibid., p.110).

Henri Bergson has written on laughter and anthropologists have studied joking relationships, but we have no comparable study of the sociology of weeping.

The emphasis on female sensibility and its channelling into tears must be set against the increasing pressures involved in being a woman. Christopher Hill provides a useful summary of these changes, and describes the position of women in his essay on Clarissa Harlowe (Hill, 1958; 1968, pp.351-76). The theme of Richardson's novel is the familiar problem of marriage and property relations. Hill, like Thomas, deals with the all-pervasiveness of the double standard and the insistence on female chastity. He writes: 'Insistence on absolute premarital chastity goes hand-in-hand with the bourgeois conception of absolute property, immune alike from the king's right to arbitrary taxation and the church's divine right to tithes (ibid., p.367). The eighteenth century saw the increasing subjugation of marriage to financial considerations and Hill comments that 'Marriage by purchase stimulates sex-war, as in Restoration comedy' (ibid., p.358). However, with the coming of industrialization women were faced with yet further problems:

> The workshop was separated from the home. In factories,
> however atrociously female labour was sweated women
> began to enjoy an equality in exploitation with men. But
> the wife in the lower-middle class family became less a help-
> meet in the business and more tied to domestic duties.
> Among new upper-middle class she became a sentimentalized
> angel of the home excluded from all other interests, a lady of
> leisure and a novel reader. Economic, legal and religious
> development combined to depress the status of these women
> (ibid., p.370).

Meanwhile their male counterparts luxuriated in a malady described as hypochondriasis. For the most part this condition was treated with respect and sympathy. Scornful allusions to it only creep in occasionally. Mrs Thrale's description of Mr Seward, a young friend of Dr Johnson's, is one such example: 'He has the misfortune to be a hypochondriac, so runs about the world to borrow spirits and to forget himself. But after all if his disorders are merely imaginary, the imagination is disorder sufficient and I am sorry for him. However, for the most part derision is reserved for female disorders.

The spread of hysteria must be set against this background of emotional refinement and increasing social and economic restraints. Whilst the men of the nation succumbed to hypochondriasis or what was later dignified with the name of The English Malady, women were plagued with – and plagued others with – hysteria. Hysteria reached its apotheosis in the nineteenth-century hysterical paroxysm. The most systematic treatment of this is to be found in Robert Brudenell Carter's *On the Pathology and Treatment of Hysteria* (1853). Throughout it is wary of feminine wiles and whims.

Carter worked in Leytonstone and his book is based on his experiences in general practice. His ideas depart in many ways from earlier accounts and are, therefore, worth presenting in full. Carter starts his treatise by cautioning against the inexactitude with which the term hysteria is used. The definition which he offers of hysteria is:

> a disease which commences with a convulsive paroxysm commonly called 'hysteria'. This paroxysm is witnessed under various aspects, and in various degrees of severity, being limited, in some cases, to a short attack of laughter or sobbing; and in others, producing very energetic involuntary movements, maintained during a considerable time, and occasionally terminating in a period of catalepsy or coma (1853, pp.2-3).

Carter goes on to describe the workings of emotion and

> the natural tendency of an emotion to discharge itself either through the muscular, the secreting, or the sanguiferous system. It remains to examine how far the unfailing adaptiveness of nature has been displayed in the selection of these channels; and what amount of benefit results from their employment, over and above the expenditure of a force which would be injurious if retained (ibid., p.15).

It is worth noting how much Freud's early account of hysteria resembles Carter's theories. Carter's account of the expression and repression of the emotions is applied in particular to the sexual passion:

> It is reasonable to expect that an emotion which is strongly felt by great numbers of people, but whose natural manifestations are constantly repressed in compliance with the usages of society, will be the one whose morbid effects are most frequently witnessed. This observation is abundantly borne out by the facts: the sexual passion in women being that which most accurately fulfils the prescribed conditions, and whose injurious influence upon the organism is most common and familiar (ibid., pp.21-2).

Carter summarizes his argument under the following two headings:

1   That emotion is a force adequate to the production of
very serious disorders in the human frame, acting upon the
muscular, vascular, and the secreting organs, and causing
various derangements both of their structure and function – the
proclivity to its influence being greatly increased by the
operation of all debilitating agents, whether local, or general,
and by all circumstances tending to make individual parts the
subjects of attention.

2   That these derangements are much more common in the
female than in the male, women not only being more prone to
emotions, but also more frequently under the necessity of
endeavouring to conceal them (ibid., pp.25-6).

Thus Carter's theory of hysteria describes the repression of emotion
and its subsequent pathological expression in hysterical paroxysms.
Women, because they are by constitution more emotional and also
because they must discipline their feelings more than men suffer more
frequently from hysteria than do men.

If relative power of emotion against the sexes be compared in
the present day, even without including the erotic passion, it is
seen to be considerably greater in the woman than in the man,
partly from natural conformation which causes the former to
feel, under circumstances where the latter thinks; and partly
because the woman is more often under the necessity of
endeavouring to conceal her feelings. But when sexual desire is
taken into account, it will add immensely to the forces bearing
upon the female, who is often much under its dominion; and
who if unmarried and chaste is compelled to restrain every
manifestation of its sway. Man, on the contrary, has such
facilities for its gratifications, that as a source of disease it is
almost inert against him, and when powerfully excited, it is
pretty sure to be speedily exhausted through the proper
channel. It may, however, be remarked that in many cases of
hysteria in the male the sufferers are recorded to have been
'continent', a circumstance which may have assimilated the
effects of emotiveness upon them to those which are constantly
witnessed in the female (ibid., p.33).

This view of women as ravaged by sexual desire and its powerless victims, is a strange one for a mid-Victorian doctor to hold, particularly in view of other prevailing stereotypes of women as devoid of sexual feelings.

The increase in hysteria and the development of an image of woman as ensnarer of men may be related to the difficulties and delay of marriage. There are a number of conflicting views on the precise nature and extent of the difficulties of marriage for women. For example, the Bankses argue that the disinclination of men to marry early because of various economic pressures was partly responsible for the increasing number of spinsters (Banks and Banks, 1964). Similarly Cunnington writes:

> Thus in '61 *The Times* expressed the view that the increasing number of unmarried daughters in the professional classes was due to the higher standard of life and later marriage of men: A man's career is smothered by a happy marriage and a large family (1935, p.169).

This postponement in turn engenders a characteristic attitude '. . . the modern girl might be amusing to flirt with but as a permanency he preferred his club' (ibid., p.169). This theme is most ably explored by J. A. Banks in *Prosperity and Parenthood* (1954). In an important review article on the status of women in nineteenth-century England, McGregor writes of 'the wretched condition of the increasing number of women for whom almost the only socially approved occupation was a marriage denied by demographic trends' (1955, p.51). Recently the demographic disadvantage of women in the marriage market has been queried by Patricia Branca (1975). She argues that the plight of the single woman may have become more difficult to conceal with urbanization, but that, in fact, no dramatic demographic changes took place in the second half of the nineteenth century. The proportion of women marrying remained the same – at roughly 85 per cent from 1851 to 1907. However, she does concede that her figures are not class specific and that it is, therefore, impossible to disprove the increased marriage difficulties allegedly experienced by middle-class girls. Whatever the real difficulties may have been, it is quite clear that the prospect of *female redundancy* was a major preoccupation of the time. During the 1860s a number of articles appeared with titles such as 'What shall we do with our old maids?' (Cobbe, 1863), 'How to provide for superfluous women' (Boucherett, 1869), 'Why are women redundant?' (Greg, 1877) and 'Female

Industry' (Martineau, 1859). Each writer was concerned with finding a basis for female self-respect and independence, whether in marriage or work. Irrespective of whether the actual chances of marriage for a woman were good or not, such widespread discussion of women as redundant members of society would be bound to affect the self-esteem and, ultimately, the health of women.

Banks sets out to explore a related theme, namely the decline in fertility. He claims that

> the decline in family size commenced as an upper middle class phenomenon at some time in the 1860's and 1870's. It was not until some time later that the new reproductive habits began to spread amongst the less privileged groups (1954, p.5).

In *The Medical History of Contraception* (1936) Himes cites democratized birth control as responsible for the decline in fertility. However, this explanation is not adequate. Banks writes: 'Why should the upper middle classes, so indifferent to the idea of family planning before the 1870's, be willing to act upon it afterwards?' (1954, p.83). Banks goes on to describe the 1870s as the period of the Great Depression which 'spread throughout industry, bringing an atmosphere of uneasiness and insecurity into a world which had grown accustomed to thinking in terms of an ever-ascending march of Victorian progress and prosperity as an eternal, immutable law' (1954, p.12). This led to confusion and a need to find new ways of maintaining earlier standards of living. Banks argues that the middle classes felt no need to limit family size whilst their material standards were not threatened. However, once these standards were threatened family planning became essential. In the early part of the century remedies for population control were put forward for the benefit of the working classes. No middle-class writer would have supposed his writings to be in any way relevant to his own sexual behaviour. Rather, marriage was postponed until an optimum income was achieved. However, with the increasingly uncertain economic climate postponement of marriage was by itself insufficient to guarantee a desired standard of living. More radical measures had to be employed. Banks writes: 'it was from this notion of the *immorality* of imprudent marriages that the later developments of the birth-control movement made their start' (ibid., p.31). Thackeray was foremost in parodying the prudential considerations which governed marriage.

What was it that insulted Nature (to use no higher name) and prevented her kindly intentions towards them? What cursed frost was it that nipped the love that both were bearing, and condemned the girl to sour sterility, and the lad to selfish bachelorhood? It was the infernal snob tyrant who governs us all, who says, 'Thou shalt not love without a lady's-maid; thou shalt not marry without a carriage and horses; thou shalt have no wife in thy heart, and no children on thy knees, without a page in buttons and a French bonne; thou shalt go to the devil unless thou hast a brougham; marry poor, and society shall forsake thee; thy kinsmen shall avoid thee as a criminal; thy aunts and uncles shall turn up their eyes and bemoan the sad, sad manner in which Tom or Harry has thrown himself away.' You, young woman, may sell yourself without shame, and marry old Croesus; you, young man, may lie away your heart and your life for a jointure. But if you are poor, woe be to you! Society, the brutal snob autocrat, consigns you to solitary perdition. Wither, poor girl, in your garret: rot poor bachelor, in your club (Thackeray, 1887, p.117).

Many other writers of this period emphasized the importance of 'a proper time to marry'. One such, William Cowper, published a book with the telling title *Economy for the single and married by one who makes ends meet* (1845). Cowper's advice is to find 'a proper mate' and to await prudently 'a proper time to marry'. The rising standards of domestic expenditure are cited to explain the increasing emphasis put on prudential considerations. The Bankses write: 'Throughout the period under review the purchasing power of many members of the middle class rose and their sense of what was appropriate to the middle class way of life rose with it' (1964, p.71). When the financial stringencies of the last thirty years of the century are superimposed on the increasing expectations of material comfort, then the changing attitudes towards family limitations become more intelligible. During the 1870s a large number of books appeared on the advisability of limiting family size. Over a million pamphlets giving details of contraception appeared between 1876 and 1891. Thus, during the latter half of the century married and family life became increasingly precarious; neither marriage nor children could be taken as a woman's rightful due.

This ambivalent attitude towards female sexuality is no doubt fostered by the difficulties encountered by women in entering marriage and within it. Carter describes sex-craving women luring the innocent and unsuspecting young physician to an improper and unnecessary use of the speculum; yet during the same period woman is presented as a public monument equipped in crinoline and inaccessible to male advances. Further ambivalence is to be found in the writings of William Acton. This ambivalence is apparent in his handbook *The Functions and Disorders of the Reproductive Organs*:

> I believe I have already mentioned the fact that the intellectual qualities are in an inverse ratio to the sex appetites. It would seem as if the two were in some degree incompatible; the inordinate exercise of the one annihilating the other. We meet with a large proportion of unmarried men among the intellectual, and some of the ablest works have been written by bachelors. Newton and Pitt were single, Kant disliked women . . (Acton, 1865, p.48).

This inverse relationship between sexual development and intellectual and moral development provides the basic theme around which subsequent ideas about female sexuality and male intellectual development and social attainment are elaborated. For example, Acton writes that

> All experience tends to prove that if a man observes strict continence in thought as well as deed, and is gifted with ordinary intelligence he is more likely to distinguish himself in liberal pursuits than those who are incontinent, whether in the way of fornication or by committing marital excess (ibid., p.49).

In fact the obstetric section of the British Medical Association (BMA) at Bath in 1878 spoke of 'sexual fraudulency' and 'conjugal onanism'. Given this general interpretation of sexuality it is not surprising that since feminine nature is, at its best, the essence of refinement and susceptibility, women must, therefore, be denied both sexual feelings and their expression. This leads to Acton's notorious claim that the average, healthy woman does not experience sexual feelings and submits to sexual advances only in so far as these are subservient to the maternal instinct. However, such refinement and sexual continence are confined to middle-class women, for women of the labouring classes are thought to be wanton and sexually depraved. This theme is elaborated at great length in Acton's treatise on *Prostitution considered in its moral, social and sanitary aspects* (1857). The double face of Victorian sexual morality has, of course, been much documented. However, the contradictory attitudes towards female sexuality and its explicit association with hysteria are less familiar. .

A later expression of the dangers of female sexuality and the attendant emotional vulnerability and mental instability is to be found in the debate concerning menstruation and higher education for women in the late nineteenth century summarized in an article called 'Victorian Women and Menstruation' (Showalter and Showalter, 1973, pp.38-44). During the last quarter of the nineteenth century it was widely held that menstruation was a pathological condition. It was seen as 'proof of the inactivity and atrophy of the uterus' (Bullough and Voght, 1973, p.67). In 1861 a German physician argued that 'there was a mechanical stimulus of nerves by the growing follicle which was responsible for congestion and menstrual bleeding' (ibid., p.68). The obvious development of these ideas was to insist on the avoidance of stimulation and excitement for women in order to decrease pathological menstruation. These ideas lent themselves readily to the subjugation of women and provided an effective deterrent to their emancipation. There were sound 'scientific' grounds for maintaining that a woman's place is in the home. During the 1870s in particular a number of writers emphasized the strains imposed by education on pubertal and adolescent females: 'in large part because of the strains which puberty and ovulation put upon them' (ibid., p.69). Women apparently could not enjoy health and education, since according to a Harvard Professor of Medicine, Edward H. Clarke, the system cannot do two things well at the same time (Clarke, 1874). Women must, therefore, if they are to be good wives and mothers, concentrate on developing their reproductive system. If such duties are not attended to at the appropriate time, reproductive development is irrevocably hindered. Therefore, 'during the growth of the female reproductive system, brain work must be avoided'. More specifically Henry Maudsley argued that intellectual activity in women diverted blood to the brain which would otherwise have succoured the reproductive organs (Maudsley, 1874). Similarly, T. S. Clouston, a Scottish physician and author of *Hygiene of the Mind* (1906), claimed that over stimulation of the female brain causes stunted growth, nervousness, headaches and neuralgias, difficult childbirth, hysteria, inflammation of the brain and insanity. The female character is likewise altered by education; the educated woman becomes cultured, but 'Is unsympathetic; learned, but not self denying' (Clouston, 1906, p.72).

Maudsley too painted an unappetizing picture of the educated woman:

It will have to be considered whether women can scorn delights and live laborious days of intellectual exercise and production, without injury to their functions as the conceivers, mothers and nurses of children. For it would be an ill thing, if it should so happen that we got the advantages of a quantity of female intellectual work at the price of a puny, enfeebled and sickly race (Maudsley, 1874, pp. 471-2).

Indeed, Maudsley transferred the debate about women and higher education to the pages of the *Fortnightly Review* (1874, pp.466-83). There he argued in the following terms: 'Male organization is one and female organization is another and come what may in the way of assimilation of female and male education and labour, it will not be possible to transform a woman into a man' (ibid., p.466). His arguments are expressed in the same vocabulary as that used to discuss lunacy. Women cannot 'choose but to be women, cannot rebel successfully against the tyranny of organization' (ibid., p.468). Given the different female organization 'There must be a difference in the method of education of the two sexes answering to differences in their physical and mental natures' (ibid., p.471). And his final summing up of the intellectual woman is that 'in the worst event they will not have been without their use as failures' (ibid., p.478). The next issue of the *Fortnightly Review* contains a splendidly eloquent and reasoned reply by Elizabeth Garrett Anderson. She complains of the difficulties of meeting Maudsley's charges on account of their vagueness. What does 'Women cannot choose but to be women' mean? And she argues that

So far as education is concerned it is conceivable and indeed probable that were they ten times as unlike as they are, many things would be especially good for both . . . if the pace be moderate, there would seem to be no good reason why the special physiological functions of women should prevent them from eating beef and bread with as much benefit as men (ibid., p.584).

And in passing she points out that labouring women are not spared their chores because of their reproductive functions. She believes that women become ill through inactivity rather than through strenuous work. She replies to Maudsley's question: 'Is it well for women to contend on equal terms with men for the goal of men's ambition?' by answering:

> Hitherto most of the women who have 'contended with men for the goal of men's ambition' have had no chance for being the worse for being allowed to do so on equal terms. They have all had the benefit of being heavily handicapped (ibid., pp.588-9).

She ends her reply on a surprisingly modern and perceptive note: namely, that physiologically based arguments about social and educational policies are the same whether they are applied to Negroes, agricultural labourers or women; they all aim to restrict opportunities for that particular social category. It is worth remembering that the enfeebling effects of education for women were emphasized precisely at a time when women were demanding higher education and other rights. The repressive effects of medical arguments make sense in this context.

Thus the emphasis on female vulnerability and pathology increased with the increasing articulateness of women and their demand for emancipation. By the turn of the century an explicit association was made between the education of women and increased risk of insanity. Dr Ralph Parsons writing in the *New York Medical Journal* in 1907 cites the fact that in 1902 42 per cent of the women admitted to New York insane asylums were well educated, whilst only 16 per cent of the men admitted had gone beyond grade school. His conclusion is that 'women who have undergone higher education are much more liable to become victims of insanity than men of the same class' (quoted in Bullough and Voght, 1973, p.75). Women's reproductive role precludes her from intellectual activity which she engages in at the risk of insanity. A synthesis of Darwinian and Spencerian thought came to be influential whereby all sorts of 'natural' female attributes were explained by their relevance to the survival of the species.

Thus, throughout two centuries female sexuality was seen as an ambiguous and dangerous force predisposing women to insanity. This review of ideas about female sexuality can be compared with the ideas developed by L. N. Rosenthal in her paper on the definition of female sexuality among Gujerati-speaking Indians of Johannesburg (1977). She considers the position of women and ideas about their sexuality. Although Gujerati women have low status, they are thought to be highly sexed and therefore destructive of male strength and dangerous to them. This suggests that low social status of women is correlated with the absence of sexual rights rather than being directly correlated with the definition of what constitutes female sexuality. This conclusion contrasts with the ideas of many feminist writers. Simone de Beauvoir, for example, maintains that there is a relationship between the downgrading of female sexuality and the inferior status of women in society.

In the final summary of her paper Rosenthal writes:

> I would like to return to the contention of de Beauvoir and other writers who have maintained that the subordinate status of women in European and American society is related to a view of their sexuality as being weak and passive, and the belief that their sexual needs are less than those of men. Among the Gujerati speaking Indians of Johannesburg, as I have shown, women are regarded as sensual creatures and their need for sexual satisfaction is recognized. Yet their status is unequivocally subordinate to that of men (ibid., p.209).

Her paper shows that it is not the definition of sexuality as such which is related to status, but the uses to which it is put. The effect of the Gujerati view of sexuality is to surround 'women with a web of restrictions' (ibid., p.209). Similarly, it would be misleading to say that there was an outright denial of female sexuality in Victorian England. The Victorian position with regard to women's sexuality is much better described as fear. Women's sexuality was regarded as dangerous and male ambivalence to it was expressed by the ease with which unsullied purity could be transformed into wanton depravity. Throughout the period covered by this essay women were considered as labile and peculiarly vulnerable and these qualities are thought to stem from the demands made upon their intellect by their sexual and reproductive activities. Even in Victorian England the dangers of female sexuality do not disappear. In the medical literature women are seen as unmanageable precisely because their status is a dependent and inferior one and they are, therefore, in need of management. High status and independent persons are never thought of as being unmanageable. Carter's view of the devious hysterical female completely contradicts the sexless stereotype of womanhood typically attributed to the Victorians. Similarly, the view of working-class women being socially dangerous contradicts the popular image held of Victorians and their attitudes towards female sexuality. Thus the critical features of the image of woman are social dependence and inferior status, sexual dangerousness and unmanageability and emotional instability arising from her sexual and reproductive role. Perhaps the brief period during which an uneasy sexual innocence has been imputed to women can be attributed to the degree of mastery which the rising male section of the bourgeoisie exercised over its womenfolk.

7
Pauper lunacy

Parliamentary reports are one index of the growth of concern about lunacy. The number of Bills, reports of select committees and inquiries relating to lunacy rose from a mere handful in the eighteenth century to 71 between the years 1801 and 1844. In part, the growth of public concern about the plight of the lunatic was encouraged and given voice and direction by Lord Ashley, later Earl of Shaftesbury. Of all the objects of his reforms, the lunatic moved him most – so much so that contemporaries hinted at some hidden pathology to explain his reformist zeal. Florence Nightingale, for example, said of him: 'Lord Shaftesbury would have been in an asylum had he not devoted himself to reforming them.' The Lunacy Act of 1845, which made the building of county asylums for the pauper insane compulsory, was passed largely due to his efforts. Indeed, it cost him much personal anguish. In a speech to the House of Commons, delivered on 6 June 1845, Ashley made the following solemn declaration: 'It is our duty to deliberate on these things . . . here we are sitting in deliberation today and tomorrow we may be the subjects of it.' And an entry in his diary for 30 June of the same year reads: 'Never have I suffered more anxiety than on these lunacy bills. I dream every night and pass in my visions, through every clause, and confuse the whole in one great mass.' It certainly cannot be said that lunacy provided indifferent ground for reforming enterprise. It was a matter very close to the reformer's heart. The Act was inspired by a recognition that large numbers of lunatics were confined in workhouses where treatment was non-existent and where potentially curable cases of lunacy were transformed into cases of incurable lunacy. It was prompted above all by an emphasis on the need for early treatment.

(In fact, the importance attributed to early treatment explains Shaftesbury's opposition to the introduction of more comprehensive safeguards for the liberty of the subject.) Shaftesbury regarded the legalization of insanity as representing a threat to the early treatment of mental illness. Thus it was only after his death that the Lunacy Consolidation Bill ('the triumph of legalism') could become law in 1890.

During this same period of increasing concern about the lack of medical facilities for the pauper insane, popular imagination was haunted by the fear of illegal detention. Many accounts of confinement in an asylum and brutal treatment were published throughout the nineteenth century by patients claiming to have been wrongfully detained. Mitford describes the notorious Warburton madhouses in London: 'If a man comes in here mad, we'll keep him so; if he is in his senses, we'll soon drive him out of them' (1823, part 1, p.1). Richard Paternoster provides another exposé of wrongful confinement in *The Madhouse System* (1841). However, the most famous and lucid account is *Perceval's Narrative* (1838). John Perceval was the fifth son of Stanley Perceval, the Prime Minister who was murdered by a lunatic in 1812. Perceval was confined in two private madhouses: Brislington House, Gloucestershire, and Ticehurst in Sussex. After his release Perceval described his asylum experiences in his *Narrative*. Perceval has little good to say of either institution. Writing of Brislington House, Perceval claims he was subjected to much degradation at that 'Madhouse, for to call that, or any like that, an asylum is cruel mockery and revolting duplicity' (1838, p.91). And later he claims that 'the humanity of the asylum consisted in the conduct of the patients not in that of the system and its agents.' At the same time we are told by one of the leading authorities on nineteenth-century private madhouses that: 'This establishment was one of the most reputable provincial licenced houses in the early nineteenth century and was, undoubtedly, the finest of the small number of purpose built houses' (Parry-Jones, 1972, p.112). The proprietor was a Quaker called Edward Long Fox of enlightened views and one of the leading physicians in the West Country. He had Brislington House built for the then astronomical sum of £35,000. Parry-Jones states that: 'Perceval was, undoubtedly, acutely psychotic at the time of his admission to Brislington House. He remained deluded and hallucinated for some time and it would appear that, at times, his behaviour was negativistic and resistive' (ibid., p.230). It may well be true that Perceval was psychotic on his admission to Brislington House, but I think one should be cautious about dismissing outright his perspective on the madhouse system as the result of a 'negativistic and resistive' disposition.

It is interesting that 1845 is the year of Shaftesbury's greatest triumph represented by the passing of the Lunacy Act and also the year in which Perceval formed The Alleged Lunatic's Friend Society to help those who, like himself, claimed to have been wrongfully committed. The Society Perceval founded aimed to

> stir up an intelligent – and active sypathy, on behalf of the most wretched, the most oppressed, the only helpless of mankind, by proving with how much needless tyranny they are treated – and this in mockery – by men who pretend indeed their cure, but who are in reality, their tormentors and destroyers
> (Perceval, 1838, p.2).

Shaftesbury saw the passing of the Lunacy Act, which made compulsory the building of county asylums, as a major achievement and Perceval's Society as a threat to early treatment which the Act hoped to encourage. Conversely, Perceval saw his Society as a major reform and defence against the growing threat presented by asylum expansion.

John Clare's medical history presents similar contradictions and queries. Clare, the poet, entered High Beech private madhouse in Essex in 1837. The proprietor, Matthew Allen, was a physician of considerable repute, well-connected and author of a respected treatise *Essays on the Classification of the Insane* (1831). Allen's emphasis on the therapeutic value of voluntary confinement is particularly interesting. Writing in 1840 of Clare's much improved condition at High Beech he says:

> He was exceedingly miserable, every instant bemoaning his poverty, and his mind did not appear so much lost and deranged as suspended in its movements by the oppressive and permanent state of anxiety, and fear, and vexation, produced by the excessive flattery at one time and over-exertion of body and mind, and no wonder that his feeble bodily frame, with his wonderful native powers of mind, was overcome.
> · I had then not the slightest hesitation in saying that if a small pension could be obtained for him, he would have recovered

instantly and most probably have remained well for life
(Tibble and Tibble, 1932, p.384).

As it turned out John Clare was not found a pension and the last
twenty-seven years of his life were spent in an asylum. His
biographers, the Tibbles, sum up the situation succinctly: 'Worry and
penury at home had planted the seeds of those delusions and brought·
him to the verge of mental and physical breakdown; absence from
home, with relief from those anxieties, supplied every condition for a
cure except one – home' (ibid., p.386). On 20 July, 1841, four years
after his arrival, Clare escaped from High Beech, thus putting an end
to his period of 'voluntary confinement'. On 29 December 1841, he
was certified insane and removed from his cottage to Northampton
General Lunatic Asylum. Here again there are conflicting reports of
the nature of his medical career. For example, in 1845 the asylum
superintendent, Prichard, writes as follows: 'He enjoys perfect liberty
here and passes all his time out of doors in the fields or town,
returning home only to his meals and bed' (ibid., p.421). But in the
same year we find Clare writing to his wife Patty: 'This is an English
Bastille . . . where harmless people are trapped and tortured till they
die – English bondage more severe than the slavery of Egypt and
Africa' (ibid., p.421). His biographers make the somewhat
superfluous comment that 'He had not yet reconciled himself to his
fate.' In fact, nearly all his letters follow a similar vein. A letter to his
children dating from 1843 complains: 'I am in a prison on all sides
that even numbs common sense. I can be civil to none but enemies
here, as friends are not allowed to see me at all' (ibid., p.420). One of
the last pieces of written communication that we have from him is a
letter in response to an inquiry about him from a Mr Jas Hipkins.
Clare's reply, dated 8 March 1860, is a moving statement of his
condition:

> Dear Sir, I am in a Madhouse and quite forget your name and who
> you are. You must excuse me for I have nothing to communicate
> or tell of, and why I am shut up I don't know. I have nothing to say
> so I conclude.
>   Yours respectfully,
>   John Clare (ibid., p.435)

Again, as in the case of Perceval's medical history, there is a
considerable discrepancy between the official, institutional version of

the truth and the truth as experienced by the recipients of care and treatment.

Finally worth mentioning is Charles Reade's novel *Hard Cash. A Matter of Fact 'Romance* first published in 1863 in Charles Dickens's weekly journal *All the Year Round.* In this novel interest in inheritance leads to the hero's unjust confinement in a madhouse. The theme is a familiar one to nineteenth-century readers. The earlier Gothic novel *Melmoth, the Wanderer* is constructed around a similar theme (Maturin, 1820). However, the peculiar interest of *Hard Cash* lies in its claims to be a faithful portrayal of reality. In fact, a reviewer for *The Times* warned readers against taking the novel too literally:

the incautious reader is apt to imagine mad doctors to be scientific scoundrels, lunatic asylums to be a refined sort of Tophet, and the visiting justices to be a flock of sheep. This is the untruthful exaggeration of fact jumbled with fiction (*The Times*, 2 January 1864).

A number of well known figures are portrayed in the novel: among them is Dr Conolly the champion of moral management and non-restraint who appears in the novel as Dr Wycherley. Now, whilst no great store can be set by a fictional presentation, it nevertheless introduces a slight query or hesitation in accepting the hitherto undisputed public image of the revolutionary doctor. Dr Conolly was seen as one of the pioneers of moral management. In 1856 his book *The Treatment of the Insane Without Mechanical Restraints* was published. He himself was a superintendent at the large lunatic asylum of Hanwell where, within a few weeks of taking over, he totally abolished all restraint. His ideas have been described above in Chapter 4.

These examples certainly show contradictory views of the condition of lunacy in England in the nineteenth century. Is one version more representative of attitudes towards insanity and the care of the insane, or are both true, and if so, how can they be reconciled? In order to answer these questions we must look more closely at the treatment of the poor.

The early nineteenth century is associated with the more humane treatment of the insane. Moral management offered the promise of cure through kindness and persuasion. Physical restraint was completely abandoned or reduced to a minimum. However, during the same period the public became sensitive to the horrific abuses

1 The Hanwell
Asylum

2   Interior of a Lunatic Asylum; from Grant, *Sketches in London,* 1838

The Portfolio,

OF

AMUSEMENT AND INSTRUCTION

IN

History, Science, Literature, the Fine Arts, &c.

No. 116.]   SUPPLEMENTARY NUMBER.   [Price 3*d*.

PATHETIC TALE OF MAD MARY.

> *Tul.* Away! thou'rt mad.
> *Sex.* I've privilege for *that—*
>   I've *been in love.*
>   *Cumberland's Elder Brutus*, Act. i, Sc.2.

How sweet is the mother's smile when she beams over her new-born infant! How cruel the hour when she must cast him into the flood, and take away the life of her first-born ; the innocent creature of beautiful, but illicit love. . . . . Die, my son; die once for all, to escape a thousand deaths!
Songs of the Madagascars.

' Who is she, with her basket of osier filled with May blossoms of Flora, where the infant joyous flowers of spring smile at each indolent passenger, and deepen the air with their wild and mellifluent fragrance ?'

See how her hands, once soft as the down of the eider, and fine as the pearl of Asia; but now, hardened and dark with the work of adversity and time ;—see how her hands run thro' the sweet mazes of her basket, wreathing the luxuriant gems into bouquets of her fancy. She is seated, surrounded by her delicate wares, on the steps of a towering mansion frowning in cold splendour at her artless doings.

Hark ! she is singing some lines of her own mad creation ;

   ' Blooming beings, blooming beings,
     People of the grassy glade,
     Sunny beings, sunny beings,
     As a shadow ye all fade,

No. 116.'—N.S.

4 A Ward in Bethlehem Hospital, c.1860

5 St Luke's Hospital, London, for the Insane by Rowlandson

9 Melancholy and Raving Madness. Figures over the Gateway
of Bethlehem Hospital

10   Workroom, Bethlehem Hospital. From the *Illustrated Times,*
1860

11 Bethlehem Hospital,
1735. From *The
Rake's Progress* by
Hogarth

12 Photographic
portrait of Henry
Maudsley, 1881.
In the Wellcome
Institute

13 Interior of The Retreat, York. From G. A. Tucker,
    Lunacy in Many Lands, n.d., p.1060

14 The douche; a method for calming violent lunatics, nineteenth century. From *Ciba Symposium,* 1950, *11,*p.1230

15 Appliances for the restraint of the insane in the Wellcome Museum

16 *The Night Mare.* Lithograph by M. Z. D. Schmid, c.1800, in the Wellcome Institute

17 Etching; scene showing people attending an exhibition of caricatures, implicitly compared with people visiting Bedlam (?). *A Visit to Bedlam,* by Richard Newton, 1794. From E. G. O'Donoghue, *The Story of Bethlehem Hospital,* London, Fisher Unwin, 1914, f.p.239

18   Machine used for calming violent lunatics, eighteenth century.
From *Ciba Symposium,* 1950, *11,* p. 1227

19   Rotatory motion machine for treatment of the insane.
From A. Morison, *Cases of Mental Disease,* London,
Longman & Highley, 1828

20 The Physiognomy
of Madness.
From Charles
Bell, *Essays on
the Anatomy of
Expression in
Painting,*
London,
Longman *et al.,*
1806, p.153

21 Lithograph
portrait of John
Conolly by
T. M. Baynes
after a painting
by R. Kirkby.
Hullmandel, n.d.;
in the Wellcome
Institute

22 Jack Sheppard visits his mother in Old Bedlam. Illustration drawn by George Cruickshank for W. H. Ainsworth's novel, *Jack Sheppard,* 1839. From E. G. O'Donoghue, *The Story of Bethlehem Hospital,* London, Fisher Unwin, 1914, f.p.239

23   Ward in Bethlehem Hospital about 1745. Engraving (n.d.)
from D. H. Tuke, *Chapters in the History of the Insane,
London,* 1882

24 Original Building of The Retreat, York. Instituted 1792. From D. H. Tuke, *Chapters in the History of the Insane, London,* 1882

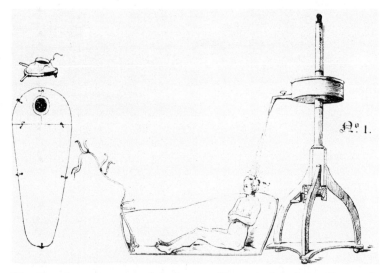

25 Douche treatment of the insane. From A. Morison, *Cases of Mental Disease,* London, Longman & Highley, 1828

within asylums. Throughout the eighteenth century there had been a number of isolated scandals to do with madhouses. However, little was done to change these appalling conditions.

During the nineteenth century shocking conditions were uncovered and described in many of the large public asylums and smaller licensed houses. The discovery and publicization of the conditions of lunatics exemplified Victorian philanthropy at its best. The condition of lunacy in England was brought to public notice as a result of the persistent efforts of a few individuals. The succession of parliamentary reports published on the subject in the first half of the nineteenth century (1808, 1815, 1828, and 1844) relied on the evidence of such self-appointed investigators of lunacy. As a result of the testimonies of these philanthropists reforms were introduced which made compulsory the erection of public asylums and the inspection of all asylums, whether public or private. The provision of lunatic asylums was prompted partly by the moral outrage felt upon the discovery of the revolting and inhumane conditions endured by the insane and partly by the newly found faith in the possibility of cure. These conditions continued with the growing needs of an industrialized population unable to cope with its incapacitated members and they account for the sudden growth of lunatic asylums. However, these institutions were found to be inadequate almost before they had been built. First, they proved to be too small: however generous the estimates of the number of beds needed per county, it was soon found that demand far exceeded supply. The size of the lunacy problem grew to fit the provisions made for it. Second, and perhaps more importantly, the asylums failed to fulfil their initial therapeutic promise. The cures which were supposed to follow from th : early detection of lunacy and asylum-based care simply did not take place. Both these problems were recognized in the parliamentary report of 1844, that is, a year before the act making compulsory the building of county asylums had been passed. In other words, the asylum system ran into trouble even before it had got going.

In the face of these difficulties it is interesting to see what remedies were proposed. The asylum was recommended in order that lunatics would be recognized as a distinct category and given specialist treatment. The dangers and disadvantages of indiscriminate mingling with other categories of deviants was emphasized. In particular, the shocking conditions in workhouses were noted. However, when problems developed, a return to the workhouse was advocated. It was thought that the asylum was functioning badly because of the unpromising human material with which it had to deal and not because of any defects intrinsic to the system. Cures did not take place because the patients admitted to asylums were incurable. The solution suggested was the return of incurables to the workhouse – precisely the state of affairs which had earlier aroused so much horror. Within a short space of time the wheel had come full circle. This chapter examines in more detail how these changes came about.

The problems of lunacy were closely related to pauperism as 75 per cent of the insane came under the Poor Law Authorities, and the great increase in the lunatic population occurred among pauper, not private patients (see, for example, Hodgkinson, 1966, pp. 138-54). One of the best accounts of the development of a psychiatry for the poor is to be found in Andrew Scull's doctoral thesis *Museums of Madness* (1974). The central problem which Scull examines is the 'transition from a type of society in which responsibility for social deviants rested primarily with the family and local community to one dominated by centrally directed intervention, by formal bureaucratic agencies of social control' (ibid., p.2). Until the early nineteenth century there was little separate provision for lunatics. The financial costs of providing for them were high and are, therefore, in some need of explanation. Scull writes: 'The successful capture of such a group by the medical profession and the large-scale and costly construction of mental hospitals in which to incarcerate them must be seen as an inherently problematic phenomenon' (ibid., p.7). Why were people willing to spend large sums of money on a hitherto neglected and abused section of the population? Proposals for the design of madhouses show the willingness of many to allocate public funds for the insane (see, for example, Report of the Select Committee on Madhouses, 1815, pp.361-70). Scull suggests that the answers are to be found by looking at the processes of industrialization and urbanization. Once the move to large towns had begun, families were no longer willing to look after unproductive or difficult family members. Thus different attitudes to the care and treatment of the insane emerged. However, it does not follow that previously the insane were indistinguishable from other categories of deviants as Andrew Scull, Kathleen Jones and other writers have supposed. Insanity is not a by-product of capitalism nor of industrialization. Scull's account rightly relates the growth of institutional care to the constraints imposed on family life by an increasingly urbanized and industrialized society. However, he is wrong to imply that institutional arrangements determine diagnostic categories and beliefs about madness, although they do, of course, influence them. His claim that insanity did not exist as a distinct category before the nineteenth century is part of his more general approach to the subject – beliefs and values are given a secondary role and are seen as being dependent on social practices. This is to undervalue the force of beliefs. Furthermore, Scull's interpretation of the reform movement as a response to industrialization and as the result of a desire on the part of asylum doctors to create a speciality for themselves, neglects the professed goals of humanitarianism and benevolence of the reformers themselves. Scull writes:

> For many centuries though, the medical approach to lunacy had been ignored in favour of the theological or demonological perspective. To a certain extent, then, the attempt to assert medical control was a novel phenomenon. Physicians had been placed in charge of the Bethlem Hospital only from the end of the sixteenth century onwards. Since none of these men published any books on insanity or made any claims to provide effective therapy, their impact in promoting the medical cause was minimal . . . For much of the first half of the eighteenth century, James Munro (1680-1752) the physician at Bethlem, was almost the only doctor in and around London who treated the mentally ill (Scull, 1974, pp.62-3).

This is an over-simplified view which ignores the large volume of medical writing on nervous maladies. For example, many books appeared on the spleen – this was commonly recognized as a nervous disorder and it was extremely widespread. However, no separate institutions were set up to care for those suffering from the spleen. Those in charge of lunatic asylums did not write about the condition of the patients in their care, neither did they seek to apply the literature on nervous disorders to them. The changes which took place in the early nineteenth century relate to the treatment of the insane and the growth of asylums rather than to theories of insanity. And Scull is surely right in attributing the capture and institutionalization of the pauper lunatic to the demands of an increasingly urbanized and industrialized society.

The Vagrancy Act 1744

The beginnings of public concern about lunacy date from the eighteenth century. At the turn of the century Defoe wrote a *Review of the State of the English Nation* (1706, pp.353-6), in which he pointed to the abuses to which the asylum might be put. Unwanted wives or rich relatives could be removed on the pretence of insanity. Throughout the century periodicals such as the *Gentleman's Magazine* unearthed and published accounts of persons unlawfully put away. These isolated scandals paved the way for a more systematic interest in the plight of the insane. The Vagrancy Act of 1744 first made separate mention of lunatics. Section 20 of that Act makes the following point:

> It shall and may be lawful for any two or more Justices of the Peace where such lunatic or mad person shall be found, by warrant under their hands and seals, directed to the constables, churchwardens and overseers of the poor of such Parish, Town or Place, to cause such persons to be apprehended and kept safely locked up in some secure place as such Justices shall appoint; and (if such Justices find it necessary) to be there chained.

Kathleen Jones says of the Act that 'The sole achievement lay in the fact that some of those suffering from mental disorder were for the first time recognised as requiring treatment' (1972, p.28). However, various treatments were already advocated and in use during the eighteenth century. The 1744 Act embodied a new emphasis on the need for institutionalization of certain categories of the insane. The Act of 1774 for the regulation of private madhouses was explicit in not making provision for pauper lunatics. Thus, although the Vagrancy Act had provided a means for the institutionalization of the insane, no subsequent legislation appeared to safeguard their health and interests. Moreover, in private madhouses there were no penalties for maltreatment. Scull rightly sums up by saying that

> the situation of the growing numbers of lunatics incarcerated in asylums and madhouses, as well as those confined in workhouses and local gaols, was to provide a ready target for the efforts of the humanitarian reformers of the next generation (1975, p.68).

Industrialization and urbanization

Industrialization and urbanization put the poor into a particularly difficult position. The poor were no longer in a dependent and, therefore, protected position. Wage earners had no possibility of safe-guarding against fluctuations in the economy and could no longer fall back on the charity of their social superiors. In these circumstances it became particularly difficult to care for an incapacitated member, the insane included:

> While the family based system for caring for the insane and other types of deviants may never have worked especially well, one suspects that by the end of the eighteenth century it was likely to have been functioning particularly badly (ibid., p.89).

Another reason singled out for the inadequacy of the family-based approach is the increasing size of the problem. One estimate puts the number of persons in receipt of poor relief as high as one in nine. Given the vastness of the problem, 'the industrial elite were increasingly attracted towards an institutionally based system' (ibid., p.90).

The Select Committee of 1805

Disquiet about the condition of lunatics was first given national expression as a result of the concern of a Gloucester magistrate, Sir George Onesiphorus Paul. In 1806, Paul wrote to the Secretary of State to bring to his notice the plight of criminal and pauper lunatics. As a result a Select Committee report was published in 1807 describing the condition of pauper and criminal lunatics. Scull describes the lunacy reformers as motivated by a mixture of evangelicalism and Benthamism. Evangelicalism is described as follows:

> The atheistic tendencies of the new industrial classes, the immorality of the slave trade, widespread cruelty to children and to animals, and, of course, the treatment of the insane; all these were aspects of contemporary society which they deplored, and problems which they attacked with a characteristic vigour and determination.
>
> Evangelicalism was at its very core a conservative movement, concerned to shore up a disintegrating social structure and a paternalistic morality against the threats posed on the one hand by an undisciplined lower class rabble, and on the other by a purely materialistic entrepreneur class (ibid., p.98).

Benthamism, by contrast was 'the creed of a class of administrators virtually created by that society' which used the principle of utility as 'a kind of primitive cost benefit analysis' (ibid., p.99). The Benthamite put an 'emphasis on providing institutional mechanisms to eliminate as well as to uncover social evils' (ibid., p.100). And this approach was particularly applicable to lunacy reform. Inspired by this mixture of evangelical zeal to uplift the lunatic and the Benthamite desire to provide an institutional solution to his problems, the Select Committee set about evaluating temporary conditions and making recommendations. Asylum-based moral management corresponded perfectly to the two guiding principles of the reformers. Their conviction was that: 'the practice of confining such lunatics and other insane persons as are chargeable to their respective Parishes in Gaols, Houses of Correction, Poor Houses, and Houses of Industry, is highly dangerous and inconvenient' (Report of the Select Committee, 1807). Moreover, the Committee asserted that those paupers whom the parish boarded out in private madhouses were well looked after. They therefore recommended that

> the measure which appears to your committee most adequate to enforce the proper care and management of these unfortunate persons and the most likely to conduce to their perfect cure, is the erection of asylums for their reception in the different parts of the kingdom (ibid.).

The following year an Act was passed recommending that each county erect an asylum for the care of the insane, and these asylums were to be supported by public funds. This Act of 1808 was a permissive one, since it had no powers to enforce its recommendations. Kathleen Jones points out that the current state of knowledge about the extent of lunacy was so vague that the Act could not but be permissive – 'the total dimensions of the need could only be guessed at'. Jones suggests two reasons for the difficulty of establishing the size of the need. First, the deficiencies of the returns sent in by each parish and, second, the desire to conceal the existence of lunacy. As an example of the unreliability of the lunacy figures, Jones cites the case of the Nottingham Asylum, the first hospital to be opened as a direct result of the 1808 Act. According to the returns, Nottinghamshire had 35 pauper lunatics. The asylum was, therefore, built with foresight to house twice as many. However, the accommodation was immediately found to be insufficient – demand far exceeded supply. An explanation which Kathleen Jones does not consider is the possible variability in the standards measuring insanity. Such a factor would also help to account for the increase in the numbers of insane once asylums had been set up. Once the asylums were there, the numbers of candidates for them increased at an ever accelerating pace. As Scull points out: 'The over-riding concern of these asylums was the security and the preservation of order within the institution' (1974, p.110). The aims of the institution were reflected in its architecture which resembled that of a prison. John Conolly, one of the moral managers, remarked that asylums

> appear to have had regard solely to the safekeeping of the inmates, and the buildings resemble prisons rather than hospitals for the cure of insanity. Even now, high and gloomy walls, narrow or inaccessible tables and benches, and prison regulations applied to the officers and attendants attest the prevalence of mistaken and limited views (1856, p.7).

However, many counties were unwilling to make the initial capital expenditure and by 1828 only nine counties had erected asylums. During this interim period the private madhouse system flourished. Asylum based treatment had become recognized and yet county asylums could not fulfil the demand which they themselves had helped to create. There was, therefore, scope for the individual entrepreneur in lunacy. Between 1807 when the Select Committee first obtained figures on the number of private madhouses in England and the report of the Metropolitan Commissioners in Lunacy of 1844, the number of private madhouses increased more than three-fold. Although as Parry-Jones has shown some madhouses provided a high standard of care and were inspired by humanitarian ideals, in others the conditions were quite revolting (1972).

The Select Committee of 1815
Increasingly criticisms were made against 'a free market in lunatics' and the Committee argued that 'some new provision of law is indispensably necessary for ensuring better care to be taken of insane persons' (1815, p.2). For the most part criticisms came from well-to-do philanthropic individuals. In fact, the report is based largely on the testimonies of these self-appointed investigators of lunatic asylums. They are well-meaning, earnest men who embody some of

the best ingredients of Victorian philanthropy, namely, scrupulous attention to detail and compassion for the destitute. Among those who testified were Godfrey Higgins, a magistrate and Governor of York Asylum, Edward Wakefield, a land agent who took it upon himself to tour licensed houses for the insane, and Henry Alexander, a banker of Ipswich who had visited many workhouses. Wakefield, for example, when asked 'have you been led in any way to examine into the treatment of insane persons?' replied: 'I have for many years been in the habit of visiting all places where I have heard they have been confined.' And to a further question: 'You have no other interest, but motives of general humanity and benevolence?' he replied: 'None whatever' (1815, p.44). Wakefield's compassionate interest is typical of many.

Godfrey Higgins prompted the investigations into York Asylum. He made charges of maltreatment of patients in the asylum. These were flatly denied. Subsequently a fire broke out under most suspicious circumstances, thus destroying any possibility of acquiring evidence of the alleged inhuman conditions. However, Higgins pursued his attack relentlessly. He found that the asylum contained a series of tiny cells measuring 8ft square, each housing several incontinent lunatics. One such cell measuring 12ft x 7ft 10in housed thirteen incontinents – Higgins found the atmosphere so offensive that he vomited.

Edward Wakefield visited Bethlem and brought the case of William Norris to the public notice. Norris had been held by a chain around his neck, the other end of which was attached to a stone wall. In this position he could neither stand nor lie flat and he had been kept in this position for nine years; not surprisingly he was totally emaciated and had contracted tuberculosis. The supposed justification for his treatment was that he had been extremely violent and had once tried to kill a keeper and another patient. However, his condition now was so weak that he was hardly likely to be able to harm anyone. Female patients were found chained to the wall either by their arm or leg. When John Haslam, the apothecary to Bethlem, was interviewed by a member of the Committee the following exchange took place:

'Would you treat a private individual patient in the same way as has been described in respect of Bethlem?'
'No, certainly not.'
'What is the difference of management?'

'In Bethlem, the restraint is by chains, there is no such thing as chains in my house.'

'What are your objections to chains and fetters as a mode of restraint?'

'They are fit only for pauper lunatics; if a gentleman was put in irons, he would not like it' (quoted in K. Jones, 1972, pp.76-7).

Clearly manacling, starving and herding naked patients together into small windowless cubicles was standard practice and thought to be perfectly fit and proper treatment.

Henry Alexander took it upon himself to inspect the quarters set aside for lunatics at forty-seven workhouses. He found nothing but 'filth, neglect and unthinking brutality' (ibid., p.82). The treatment meted out to pauper lunatics was the subject considered by the Select Committee. The following year the Committee was reassembled to consider the condition of private madhouses. Here conditions had worsened as a result of a rapid increase in the demand for institutional care for pauper lunatics. The general picture was one of

Fetters and chains, moppings at the morning toilet, irregular meals, want of exercise, the infliction of abusive words, contemptuous names, blows with the fist, or with straps, or with keys, formed an almost daily part of the lives of many unprotected beings (quoted in Scull, 1975, p.123).

The Committee members came to the conclusion that

If the treatment of those in the middling or lower classes of life, shut up in hospitals, private madhouses, or parish madhouses, is looked at, your committee are persuaded that a case cannot be found where the necessity for a remedy is more urgent (Report, 1815, p.2).

Throughout the report the conditions are described as inhuman and the patients as animal-like. In Bethlem Hospital this was particularly true: 'The patients in this room were dreadful idiots, their nakedness and their mode of confinement gave this room the appearance of a dog-kennel' (ibid., p.46).

The Select Committee of 1815-16 thus drew upon a wealth of material culled from many witnesses and relating to many different asylums, unlike the 1805 Committee which had relied upon a single witness, namely, Sir George O. Paul. When such conditions became known to the middle classes the impact was enormous. Not least as

Scull observes, because of 'the characteristic ignorance of their class concerning the living conditions which the proletariat as a whole had to endure'. Chadwick aptly summarized the relations between the two classes:

the statements of the condition of considerable proportions of the labouring population have been received with surprise by the wealthier classes living in the immediate vicinity, to whom the facts were as strange as if related to foreigners or the natives of an unknown country (ibid., p.124).

The treatment of the pauper insane, therefore, appeared doubly abhorrent and scandalous due to an ignorance of the conditions of paupers. The 1815-16 Committee produced a mass of material to shock the sensitive middle classes. Moreover, the Committee also had proposals for the cure of the evils which they had uncovered. Their first proposal was the compulsory erection of county asylums at public expense, the second was a system of public inspection to prevent abuse. The report also contained an appendix on the design of ideal asylums. Neither of these proposals were implemented for a further thirty years; this delay was due in part to the general antipathy towards centralization and in part to the reluctance to make any financial outlay.

The Select Committee of 1827
In 1827 another Select Committee was formed to inquire into the condition of Metropolitan Madhouses. This Committee was set up as a result of the investigations by Lord Robert Seymour of the notorious Warburton Madhouses in London. The evidence heard by the members of the Committee contained a by now familiar catalogue of abuses and horrors. A guardian and director of the poor of the parish of Marylebone gave the following evidence:

We found a considerable number of very disgusting objects – a description of pauper lunatics, I should conceive chiefly idiots in a very small room, and several of them were chained to the wall. The air of the room was highly oppressive and offensive, in so much so that I could not draw my breath; I was obliged to hold my breath while I stayed to take a very short survey of the room . . . it contained the description of patients called the wet patients; they were chiefly in petticoats . . . They appeared to be the worst description of decided idiots; and the room was exceedingly oppressive from the excrement and smell which existed there (Scull, 1975, p.188).

The ingredients of darkness, overcrowding, filth and stench are all there again. Moreover, witnesses testified that Warburton's Madhouses were not much worse than others in the London area. As a result of the 1827 inquiries, the County Asylums Act and the Madhouses Act were passed in 1828. Both aimed at extending national control over madhouses. The first Act demanded annual returns to the Home Department of the number of admissions, discharges and deaths; the second demanded the appointment of fifteen Metropolitan Commissioners who would be responsible for licensing and supervising madhouses within the London area. Relative to earlier aspirations of lunacy reformers, the act was modest and circumscribed in its goals. Little control was achieved over asylums outside the London area and the Act thus avoided giving offence to or curtailing the power of county magistrates. As it turned out, the Metropolitan Commissioners were highly skilled politicians who could argue their case with force and articulateness. Subsequent tours of metropolitan madhouses showed marked improvement: a return to one of Warburton's houses by Ashley found it 'extremely clean and well-ventilated . . . greatly improved' (ibid., p.196). No doubt this is an over-optimistic picture, although there clearly were improvements. Meanwhile, horrific conditions persisted in the asylums outside London. The Metropolitan Commissioners carried on the original aims of the lunacy reformers, namely to establish adequate asylum provision for all pauper lunatics and an effective means of collecting information about the condition of asylums and of enforcing the maintenance of minimum standards of care. Meanwhile the success of the moral managers and the complete removal of physical restraint at large asylums, such as Hanwell and Lincoln, provided hope that the reformers' ideals might indeed be realized.

The Report of the Metropolitan Commissioners (1844)
In 1842 Lord Granville Somerset introduced a Bill in parliament proposing an increase in the power of the Metropolitan Commissioners by granting them the right to inspect madhouses

throughout the country. This Bill became law in August of that year. The number of Commissioners was increased from fifteen to twenty and it was stipulated that they should travel about the country in pairs composed of a legal expert and a medical man. Thus detailed inspection of every asylum became possible. Two years later a report of the Metropolitan Commissioners was produced (1844). The report was comprehensive, including domestic details of the running of the asylums, with sections on the non-restraint system, the nature of insanity and the admission of pauper lunatics from workhouses and was based on visits to 166 public and private asylums. Kathleen Jones describes it

> as a muddled report in which details obtruded and the overall picture is not easily grasped. Ashley had little literary ability, but the patient piling of fact on fact provided a sound basis for the recommendations which concluded the report (1972, p.135).

From the modern reader's point of view its non-selectiveness and seemingly random approach make it particularly informative. By and large the report found that many asylums were badly sited and made inadequate provision for their inmates:

> The asylums thus brought before our view, exhibit instances of almost every degree of merit and defect. Some are constructed on an extensive scale, and combine most of the advantages and defects of a wealthy establishment. Others are mean, poor, confined within narrow bounds and almost wholly without comforts or resources of any kind. Some are situated in open and healthy places, in the midst of large airing grounds, and cheerful prospects. Others are in the centre of towns and populous suburbs, without good air and without space sufficient for daily exercise. In some places, books and amusements are furnished abundantly for the benefit of patients, and various means of occupation, adapted to their capacities and previous habits are provided. In others, the lunatic is left to pass his time listless and unoccupied only with the delusions that disturb him, and which thus, being diverted by no amusement or employment in the course of time become strengthened and not to be removed (Report, 1844, p.6).

However, the over-riding argument for more asylums was not the bad features of the existing asylum system but the optimistic faith in the possibility of cure given an early diagnosis:

> At The Retreat in York, at the Asylums of Lincoln and
> Northampton, and at the Asylum for the County of Suffolk,
> tables were published, exhibiting the large proportion of cures
> effected in cases where patients are admitted within three
> months of their attacks, the less proportion where patients are
> admitted after three months and the almost hopelessness of
> cure when persons are permitted to remain in workhouses or
> elsewhere, and are not sent into proper asylums until after a
> lapse of a year from the period when they have first been
> subject to insanity (Scull, 1974, p.209).

The views of the Commissioners were echoed by the press. The
detection of insanity in its early stages and the possibility of cure
pointed to the need for asylum treatment.

However, the report emphasized the dangers of clogging up
asylums with incurable patients, a danger particularly great in
asylums for the poor.

> These places, (even such of them as are upon the most
> extended scale) are, we regret to say, filled with incurable
> patients and are thus rendered incapable of receiving those
> whose malady might admit of cure. It has been the practice, in
> numerous instances to detain the insane pauper at the
> workhouse or elsewhere, until he becomes dangerous or
> unmanageable, and then when his disease is beyond all medical
> relief to send him to a Lunatic Asylum where he may remain
> the rest of his life, a pensioner on the public. This practice
> which has been carried on for the sake of saving, in the first
> instance, to each parish some small expense, has confirmed the
> malady of many poor persons, has destroyed the comfort of
> families, has ultimately imposed a heavy burden upon parishes
> and counties, and has, in great measure nullified the utility of
> public Lunatic Asylums, by converting them into a permanent
> refuge for the insane, instead of hospitals for their relief and
> cure (Select Committee, 1844, p.92).

Asylums are thus impeded in the proper execution of their task by the
unexpected and growing number of incurables. As early as 1834 the
resident physicians at Hanwell drew to the attention of the
magistrates 'The melancholy fact of the house being filled by old and

incurable cases' which he thought were due 'almost entirely to the neglect of proper remedies in the early stages of the disease.' (ibid., p.88). Table 1 supplied by the Metropolitan Commissioners gives the number of curable and incurable cases in asylums erected for the pauper insane:

Table 1

County Asylums			
	Curable	*Incurable*	*Total*
Bedford	27	112	139
Chester	48	116	164
Dorset	14	139	153
Kent	22	227	249
Lancaster	65	546	601
Middlesex	58	917	975
Norfolk	108	56	164
Suffolk	27	179	206
Surrey	20	362	382
York W.R.	48	384	432

County and subscription Asylums			
	Curable	*Incurable*	*Total*
Cornwall	13	120	133
Gloucester	59	198	257
Leicester	63	68	131
Nottingham	37	88	125
Stafford	48	197	245

By the middle of the century the paradoxical situation had arisen whereby asylums were not able to cure because of the large numbers of incurable patients. However, there is a difficulty in distinguishing between patients who have simply not been cured and those who are incurable. Explicit definitions of the term incurable are hard to find, even though the classification is used repeatedly. However, by and large the term is used as a synonym for the contemporary expression 'long term patient'. The 1844 Report describes an incurable as one who has been resident in an asylum for two or more years. The recommendations of the Report include the suggestion that

> separate receptacles be established for chronic cases, to be conducted in a manner adapted to the wants of the patients but upon a less expensive scale than the present County Asylums.

Thus alternative asylums are proposed to remedy the deficiencies of existing asylums.

The Report of the Commissioners was swiftly followed by two parliamentary Acts: The Lunatics Act of 1845 set up a permanent national Commission of Lunacy, empowered to visit every kind of lunatic asylum at frequent intervals. The Commission consisted of five lay members and six full-time, paid members – three doctors and three lawyers. A further Act (8 & 9 Victoria, c.126) made compulsory the building of county asylums for the provision of pauper lunatics. By 1845 the two principal goals of lunacy reform had been achieved: 'The insane had been sharply distinguished from other types of indigent and troublesome people, and the asylum had been recognized as the most suitable place for them' (Scull, 1975, p.214). Kathleen Jones sees the 1845 Act as a triumphant achievement:

Ashley and his colleagues had aroused the conscience of mid-Victorian society, and had set a new standard of public morality by which the care of the helpless and degraded classes of the community was to be seen as a social responsibility (1972, p.149).

Scull, on the contrary, sees this as an encroachment by the moral entrepreneur on the lives of individuals and lunatics in particular, and as the reification of the category of mental illness.

Both accounts capture a part of the truth. Scull's account of the expansion of the asylum is the more comprehensive and convincing. It makes sense of a wealth of disparate details, in particular the promise of cure held out by the asylums and the simultaneous growth of the asylum population which belies such a promise. The asylum came into being when notions of dependence and protection characteristic of pre-industrial society were abandoned. Insanity was seen as requiring specialist treatment, an essential feature of which was that it should be asylum-based. The first ingredient of treatment was that the patient should be removed from the setting which had first precipitated his attack, in other words, his home. This emphasis on asylum treatment in turn favoured the development of specialist asylum doctors. Scull concedes that 'at first sight, moral treatment seemed to be an unpromising basis for any profession trying to assert special competence in the treatment of the insane' (ibid., p.259). Since moral managers specifically denied the value of any medical contribution to the problem of insanity, it is difficult to see how doctors could achieve professional dominance over lunatics. However, since treatment, whether medical or not, was asylum-based, the first step to claiming professional expertise was made.

After the publication of the findings of the Select Committee of 1815 and 1816, Bills had been introduced which proposed that madhouses should be kept under surveillance by boards of inspectors to be chosen from local magistrates. Such attempts to introduce lay inspection and criticism of madhouses were clearly seen as a threat by the asylum doctors. Both Bills were vetoed by the House of Lords and for the time being the doctors' supremacy remained unscathed. During this period medical literature on insanity burgeoned. Lay control of asylums was fiercely resisted. The number of Metropolitan Commissioners was expanded to include several doctors.

> Insanity was transformed from a vague, culturally defined
> phenomenon afflicting an unknown but probably small
> proportion of the population into a condition which could only
> be authoritatively diagnosed, certified and dealt with by a
> group of legally recognised experts and which was now seen as
> one of the major forms of deviance in English society (ibid.,
> p.317).

The growth of the asylum and its failure

We return now to the contradictions which underlie any consideration of psychiatry in the nineteenth century. I have mentioned that despite the promise of cure following early detection and treatment the asylum population continued to grow. The 1844 Report was already aware of the inadequacy of asylum provision: 'It must be observed as a remarkable circumstance, with respect to counties having public pauper Lunatic Asylums, that it has been found necessary to enlarge almost every asylum of that sort that has hitherto been erected' (Report, 1844, p.84). Another paradox lies in the fact that the reformers continue to urge the expansion of the asylum system even to the extent of advocating a parallel, inferior asylum system, despite their awareness of its many shortcomings and the abuses which it encouraged. 'How were the reformers to account for the fact that the majority of asylums failed so miserably?' (ibid., p.329). Sir Robert Peel, in fact, argued that the failings of the asylums indicated that society would be better off without them:

There could not be a question that unless asylums for the
pauper lunatics were well-conducted, they would be a curse
rather than a blessing: and it would be infinitely better to have
none at all, than such as would offer temptation to send
unfortunate creatures to them. There were many cases in which
the patient was merely troublesome, and it was much better as
these should be abroad, it being preferable to leave them in the
custody of their relatives, than lock them up in madhouses
(quoted in Scull, 1974, p.342).

However, there were strong social pressures on maintaining and
expanding the asylum system which were already acknowledged in
the 1844 Report: 'A County Asylum is erected for the benefit of the
whole county and is to be considered not merely a place of seclusion
or safe custody, but as a public hospital for cure' (p.81). These social
pressures are also illustrated by the writings of Becher,
superintendent of Nottinghamshire Asylum. Becher advocated the
building of further asylums not in terms of the benefits which would
thereby accrue to patients, but in terms of the relief thereby afforded
to the community.

The services that it renders to society, are effected by removing
many sources of injury and annoyance, which are reciprocally
suffered and inflicted by those unhappy persons when
permitted to wander at large in our streets and highways; and
by relieving families from the burden and responsibility of a
painful and unavailing attendance on a disease, to which they
are utterly incapable of rendering any real assistance (Scull,
1974, p.322).

Thus asylums answered a growing need in the community to care for
unwanted deviants. With their expansion the standards of care and
physical conditions deteriorated: 'Asylum buildings became
increasingly monotonous, drearily functional, prison-like' (ibid.,
p.365). Whereas Hanwell Asylum had cost £160 per head to build,
Ashley now estimated that adequate accommodation could be
provided for curable lunatics at £80 per head, and the cost of
incurables was estimated to be still lower. Asylum attendants were
recruited from among the unemployed and disreputable sections of
other professions. Thus although the quality of care did not improve,
the asylums continued to be built and by 1847 thirty-six of the fifty-
two counties had complied with the 1845 Act and built asylums of

Table 2

Showing the proportion (per cent) of recoveries to admissions, excluding transfers, re-admissions (from 1891) on fresh reception orders rendered necessary by previous reception orders having expired under Section 38 of the Lunacy Act, 1890, and Admissions into idiot establishments; of deaths to daily average number resident

Year	Proportion (per cent) of recoveries to admissions			Averages of each five-year period			Proportion (per cent) of deaths to daily average number residents		
	Male	Female	Total	Male	Female	Total	Male	Female	Total
1873	32.46	41.34	36.96				12.27	8.26	10.16
1874	35.85	45.21	40.53				12.25	8.51	10.29
1875	36.10	42.77	39.44	34.78	42.75	38.78	13.15	8.80	10.85
1876	36.12	43.18	39.69				12.05	8.32	10.08
1877	33.39	41.25	37.30				12.03	8.01	9.00
1878	36.02	43.85	39.94				12.17	8.08	10.00
1879	37.25	43.54	40.50				12.30	8.88	10.47
1880	37.06	43.28	40.29	36.11	43.68	39.97	10.80	7.58	9.08
1881	34.85	44.46	39.72				11.33	7.43	9.24
1882	35.39	43.27	39.41				11.11	7.37	9.11
1883	34.79	42.00	38.50				11.67	7.60	9.47
1884	35.34	45.17	40.33				11.45	7.86	9.51
1885	38.14	45.56	41.99	35.55	44.47	40.11	10.70	8.24	9.37
1886	35.55	46.55	41.16				11.90	8.43	10.03
1887	33.93	43.05	38.56				11.14	8.20	9.56
1888	34.10	43.04	38.71				11.62	8.03	9.69
1889	35.57	41.78	38.81				11.59	8.00	9.65
1890	34.77	42.08	38.59	35.36	42.82	39.22	12.03	8.54	10.14
1891	37.49	44.36	41.04				12.03	8.33	10.02
1892	34.89	42.85	38.94				11.40	8.46	9.81
1893	35.04	41.63	38.45				11.33	8.34	9.71
1894	35.06	45.23	40.31				11.19	7.72	9.32
1895	34.36	41.80	33.18	35.23	42.09	38.76	11.99	8.33	10.01
1896	36.47	40.47	38.53				10.70	7.65	9.05
1897	35.24	41.31	38.35				11.36	7.81	9.43
1898	33.34	40.21	36.87				11.00	8.08	9.45

(including idiot establishments); and of recoveries to daily average number resident (excluding idiot establishments) in five-year periods, from 1873 to 1897 inclusive, and in 1898, relating to patients in county and borough asylums, hospitals, licensed houses, state asylums, and private single patients.

Year	Proportion (per cent) of recoveries to admissions			Averages of each five-year period			Proportion (per cent) of deaths to daily average number residents		
	Male	Female	Total	Male	Female	Total	Male	Female	Total
1873				9.90	11.44	10.72			
1874				11.40	12.70	12.09			
1875	12.35	8.38	10.26	11.62	12.14	11.90	11.03	11.99	11.54
1876				11.60	12.33	11.99			
1877				10.63	11.32	11.00			
1878				11.28	11.90	11.61			
1879				10.91	11.59	11.28			
1880	11.54	7.87	9.58	10.66	11.41	11.07	10.63	11.41	11.05
1881				10.20	11.31	10.80			
1882				10.09	10.84	10.50			
1883				10.18	10.88	10.56			
1884				10.04	11.03	10.58			
1885	11.37	8.07	9.59	9.76	10.49	10.16	9.70	10.61	10.20
1886				9.32	10.58	10.00			
1887				9.19	10.08	9.68			
1888				9.19	10.33	9.81			
1889				9.34	10.02	9.71			
1890	11.73	8.27	9.86	9.65	10.57	10.15	9.78	10.52	10.18
1891				10.66	11.06	10.88			
1892				10.08	10.60	10.37			
1893				9.90	10.49	10.22			
1894				9.65	11.01	10.39			
1895	11.31	7.97	9.50	9.67	10.32	10.02	9.71	10.22	9.99
1896				9.91	9.67	9.78			
1897				9.42	9.63	9.53			
1898				8.80	9.28	9.06			

Source: Taken from the 53rd Report of the Commissioners in Lunacy, 1899, pp.86-7.

their own. However, the prospects of a cure remained bleak. Scull writes: 'The predicted rise in the proportion of cures quite simply failed to occur' (ibid., p.409). Table 2 gives estimates made by the superintendents of the percentage of curable lunatics. Superintendents still attributed their lack of success to insufficiently early detection. 'Yet no matter how many new beds were provided... curable cases apparently never materialised' (ibid., p.413). Throughout the century estimates of the number of incurable patients continued to increase and the numbers of actual recoveries decreased. With the swelling numbers of incurables, pretensions to moral management of the patients were abandoned and institutions became increasingly custodial. The deterioration of treatment was matched by the increasing size of the asylum. The average size of asylums increased year by year throughout the century as Table 3 shows:

Table 3

Date	No. of asylums	Average size
1827	9	116
1850	24	297
1860	41	386
1870	51	548
1880	61	657
1890	66	802

Source: K. Jones, *Lunacy, Law and Conscience 1744-1845*, ed. W. J. H. Sprott, London, Routledge & Kegan Paul, 1955, p.116.

However, despite the increase in the size of county asylums, the size of private asylums did not increase significantly. The increase was confined to the population of pauper lunatics. The Report of the Commissioners in Lunacy for the year 1877 gives a series of very useful Tables showing the size of the lunatic population and its increase. The Commissioners claim that 'the average annual increase of the last ten years (1867 to 1876 inclusive) has been 1,755' (Report, 1877, p.2). Table 4 shows that the population of private patients increased by a very small amount whilst the population of pauper lunatics doubled (ibid., pp.8-9). The figures also show the ratio of pauper lunatics to the total population. The figures indicate that not only did the actual numbers of lunatics increase but that they also increased relative to the rapidly increasing population (ibid., pp.10-11). In turn, the huge size of asylums meant that activities of patients were increasingly routinized within asylums. Granville, in the Report of the Select Committee of 1877 wrote:

The classification generally made is for the purpose of shelving
cases; that is to say, practically it has that effect . . . in
consequence of the treatment not being personal, but simply a
treatment in classes, there is a tendency to make whole classes
sink down into a sort of chronic state . . . I think they come
under a sort of routine discipline which ends in their passing
into a state of dementia (1877, pp.396-7).

Once the asylum had been found as a solution for the insane it
continued to be used by virtue of a certain conservatism. And John
Arlidge in his treatise on the state of lunacy (1859) describes the effect
of increasing size and routinization on the inhabitants of asylums.

In a colossal refuge for the insane, a patient may be said to
lose his individuality and to become a member of a machine so
put together, as to move with precise regularity, and invariable
routine; a triumph of skill adapted to show how such
unpromising materials as crazy men and women may be drilled
into order and guided by rule, but not an apparatus calculated
to restore their pristine self-governing existence. In all cases
admitting of recovery, or of material amelioration, a gigantic
asylum is a gigantic evil and figuratively speaking a
manufactory of chronic insanity (quoted in Scull, 1974, p.102).

A separate psychiatry for the poor

The expansion of the lunatic population is particularly interesting
since it occurred almost exclusively among the pauper insane; the
number of private patients increased hardly at all. By the end of the
century the pauper insane constituted almost 90 per cent of the
asylum population. With increasing efforts at reform the numbers
estimated as insane increased: in 1810 one person in 7,300 was
estimated insane; in 1820 one person in 2,000; in 1829 one person in
769. Scull writes that

in the 45 years immediately following the establishment of a
compulsory system of public asylums for the early treatment
and cure of lunatics, while the total population had risen by a
mere 78 per cent, the number of lunatics had more than
quadrupled (1974, p.567).

How was this increase explained? Shaftesbury attributed it to improved standards of registration and observation. The Lunacy Commissioners in their annual report wrote:

> There can be little doubt that the system of observation and
> enquiry adopted of late years, however imperfect it may still
> be, has led to the detection and classification as insane, of
> many persons formerly looked upon as ordinary paupers (p.78).

However, more systematic record keeping does not account for the fact that this increase occurred largely among the pauper insane and not among private patients. Scull provides a summary of the situation: between 1844 and 1870 the number of private patients increased by about 100 per cent whilst the number of pauper lunatics increased by about 365 per cent. Table 4 taken from the annual report of the Lunacy Commissioners for 1896 shows the rate of increase in the number of private and pauper lunatics between 1859 and 1895. Why was the increase so disproportionate between these two types of patients? The answers which Scull gives seem particularly plausible. He writes: 'From the moment the asylums opened they functioned as museums for the collection of the unwanted' (ibid., p.612) and 'Asylums became a dumping ground for a heterogeneous mass of physical and mental wrecks' (ibid., p.614). He makes the very perceptive point that from the moment of their existence asylums reduce people's level of tolerance of deviants. Given that an institutional remedy is available, people are no longer willing to put up with lunatic relatives. He concludes his thesis with the following paradox:

> it remains perhaps the most paradoxical feature of the entire
> reform process that the adoption of a policy avowedly aimed at
> rehabilitation and the rise of a profession claiming expertise in
> this regard should have been accompanied by a startling and
> continuing rise in the proportion of the population officially
> recognized as insane. I have contended that this phenomenon
> cannot be explained away as merely a statistical artefact, the
> product of improved record keeping. Nor will a simplistic
> account which stresses psychiatry's imperialistic tendencies
> suffice, even though it is clear that such proclivities existed.
> The eagerness of the profession was one thing; the willingness
> of the public quite another (ibid., p.660).

Table 4

Ratio (per 10,000)		Year												
		1859	1869	1879	1886	1887	1888	1889	1890	1891	1892	1893	1894	1895
Private lunatics to population	Males	2.56	2.88	3.23	2.97	2.94	2.91	2.94	2.90	2.89	2.89	2.80	2.78	2.73
	Females	2.21	2.36	2.72	2.70	2.68	2.64	2.67	2.74	2.75	2.74	2.72	2.75	2.70
	Total	**2.38**	**2.61**	**2.97**	**2.83**	**2.81**	**2.77**	**2.80**	**2.81**	**2.82**	**2.82**	**2.76**	**2.77**	**2.71**
Pauper lunatics to population	Males	14.33	19.17	21.98	23.64	23.81	24.27	24.53	24.66	24.51	24.54	25.06	25.57	25.95
	Females	17.49	22.79	26.48	28.30	28.13	28.34	28.52	28.93	28.91	28.95	29.23	29.55	29.91
	Total	**15.95**	**21.03**	**24.29**	**26.04**	**26.03**	**26.36**	**26.59**	**26.86**	**26.78**	**26.81**	**27.21**	**27.62**	**28.00**
Criminal lunatics to population	Males	0.55	0.46	0.44	0.40	0.36	0.37	0.41	0.39	0.39	0.39	0.38	0.37	0.38
	Females	0.15	0.12	0.13	0.12	0.11	0.11	0.12	0.11	0.11	0.12	0.12	0.12	0.12
	Total	**0.34**	**(a)0.29**	**0.28**	**0.25**	**0.23**	**0.24**	**(b)0.26**	**0.25**	**0.25**	**0.25**	**0.24**	**0.24**	**0.24**
Total lunatics to population	Males	17.44	22.51	25.65	27.01	27.11	27.55	27.88	27.95	27.79	27.82	28.24	28.72	29.06
	Females	19.85	25.27	29.34	31.12	30.92	31.09	31.31	31.78	31.77	31.81	32.07	32.42	32.73
	Total	**18.67**	**23.93**	**27.54**	**29.12**	**29.07**	**29.37**	**29.65**	**29.92**	**29.85**	**29.88**	**30.21**	**30.63**	**30.95**

Source: Taken from the annual report of the Lunacy Commissioners, 1877, p.13.

Scull's interpretation of the development of lunatic asylums is given indirect support by a comparison with the growth of general hospitals. Hospitals have made a positive contribution to the care and treatment of the sick only within the last 100 years. Before that time hospitals were feared as gateways to death and only the destitute were to be found there.

> Thus illness of any kind was normally endured at home: patients who thought it efficacious purchased such medical advice and treatment as they could afford. There was a fairly clear class hierarchy of medical advisers as there was of patients (Abel-Smith, 1964, p.2).

The hospital, like the asylum, was a last resort for those who could not afford anything better. However, the failure of the asylum to provide the cure which it had promised does not altogether disqualify the move to erect county asylums and the reformist zeal which went with it. Kathleen Jones is surely right in drawing attention to the humanitarian motivation of the reformists. The men who took it upon themselves to visit asylum after asylum and to describe and publicize the abuses which they found were undoubtedly motivated by the highest ideals. The fact that these ideals were not realized within the institutional setting which they proposed does not invalidate them. But Jones's account does fail to take into account the forces operating in society and within the asylum which militated against a successful outcome. Scull's account, on the other hand, looks merely at the hidden functions of the asylum and discounts the noble ideals of the founders.

Once the reform movement got under way and the numbers of asylums increased, attention was focused on the illegal detention of patients. The actual condition of patients and the treatment meted out to them was no longer of concern. 'On the national level the select committee of 1859-60 and 1877 both of which enquired into the treatment of the insane exhibited little concern with the issue of cure (or rather the asylum's failure to cure) lower class patients' (Scull, 1975, p.448). Kathleen Jones also concurs that the issue of treatment and cure had acquired secondary importance in relation to that of illegal detention.

> In theory the committee thought that it was better to lessen legal procedures of certification and to make early treatment possible. The danger that those who needed treatment would

not get it in time was greater than the danger of illegal detention; but in practice most of their recommendations were for changes which lessen this latter danger and thereby increase the former (1972, p.160).

It seems that despite Shaftesbury's insistence on the over-riding importance of early treatment, the mood had swung the other way and the public were becoming aware of the hidden function of asylums. Shaftesbury's appeal for early treatment was made against the flow of other opinions. As a member of the 1877 Select Committee, Shaftesbury was asked: 'Do you consider that the facility with which patients are admitted to asylums is not too great at the present day?' To which Shaftesbury replied 'No, certainly not . . . we stated so in 1859 and we state it still more emphatically now.' Thus the movement for tightening up legal procedures for admission had to wait until Shaftesbury's death. The Lunacy Act of 1890 which Jones describes as the triumph of legalism went against the whole tenor of the earlier reform movement; it reflected loss of faith in the asylum and the fearful image which it had acquired in the public imagination.

Note
[1]This is now available in book form, published by Allen Lane (1979).

8
The tyranny of organization

The previous chapter documented the increase of the lunatic population. The Lunacy Commissioners estimated that the numbers of lunatics increased by 1,775 a year between 1867 and 1877. Even allowing for the sudden and continuing population increase from about 1800 onwards, the ratio of lunatics to the general population increased. As we saw, this increase was negligible among private patients and considerable among pauper lunatics. At the same time as the number of lunatics increased, the numbers of people in receipt of indoor relief also increased. Thus the growth of lunacy must be seen side by side with the growth of institutionalism generally. Demand invariably expanded to outstrip the number of beds provided. This suggests that the asylums were dealing with a social problem of growing dimensions rather than a strictly medical one.

Those concerned with lunacy were aware that the problem had assumed unmanageable proportions. Whereas earlier writing had been permeated with enthusiasm for asylum-based treatment, the Lunacy Commissioners later complained that their asylums were grinding to a halt because of the incurables. The problem therefore had to be reduced to manageable proportions, however brutal the means. As we saw, the Lunacy Commissioners, therefore, urged a separate psychiatry for the poor run with considerably less financial outlay.

Clearly, lunacy was closely related to pauperism. A brief review of the history of the poor law is, therefore, in point. The 1834 Poor Law Act was, according to the Webbs, based on 'the famous "principle" that the situation of the pauper should not be made really or apparently so eligible as the situation of the independent labourer of the lowest class' (1910, p.1). It was also based on the revolutionary principle of national uniformity in the treatment of the destitute. The workhouse test was used as a practical test whereby the principle of less eligibility could be enforced. The workhouse was made so unpleasant that no one would resort to it except as a last, desperate measure. Thus there was a strong element of punishment in the giving of poor relief. Indoor relief in the workhouse was offered as a deterrent to the able-bodied, whilst outdoor relief was only offered to the sick. However, despite the aims of the Poor Law authorities to provide indoor relief in the workhouse with a view to deterring applicants, in practice this aim was not realized. Already in the 1830s it proved too expensive to provide indoor relief and only a fraction of the destitute were accommodated in workhouses. Ruth Hodgkinson writes: 'even in the worst pauperized districts, not more than 4-5 per cent of the able-bodied could be accepted in the workhouses. In 1843 85 per cent of poor relief was domiciliary' (1967, p.147). Economic constraints determined the numbers which could be accommodated in workhouses. However, whilst outdoor relief was cheaper to provide than indoor relief, the workhouse still provided a much cheaper form of accommodation than the lunatic asylum. The average cost of building a workhouse was £40 per head, whereas the cost of building an asylum varied from £100 to £350 (see ibid., pp.147-84). Clearly, therefore, there were financial reasons for preferring the workhouse to the lunatic asylum. Indeed, financial arguments were in fact used in advocating the return of lunatics to the workhouse.

> The fall in the number of lunatic pauper inmates of workhouses in the late 'forties and their gradual disproportionate rise in the 'fifties was no doubt to a great extent caused by the considerable emptying of workhouses when the asylums were first built, and then, because they were filled, the workhouses had to receive back many of their chronic patients (ibid., p.585).

However, the nature of poor relief changed and the workhouses into which lunatics were received back had also changed. During the latter part of the century poor relief came to be increasingly centred on the workhouse. The nature of these changes was carefully noted by the Report of the Royal Commission on the Poor Laws:

the administrators of the Poor Law have been changing the character of their system. It has become more and more an indoor system. In 1871-9 the outdoor poor outnumbered the indoor poor by 4.5 to 1. In 1896 to 1905 this proportion had been reduced to 2.6 to 1 (1909, p.50).

They give the data shown in Table 5 which records the number of indoor and outdoor paupers.

Table 5

Between	Decrease in mean no. of outdoor paupers	Increase in mean no. of indoor paupers
1871-9 and 1880-7	64,591	28,124
1880-7 and 1888-95	26,833	9,188
1888-95 and 1896-1905	3,035	27,585

Source: Report of the Royal Commission on the Poor Laws, 1909, p.50.

Thus between the 1870s and 1880s there occurred the largest increase in the average number of indoor paupers and the largest decrease in the average number of outdoor paupers relieved. The Webbs write: 'From about 1871 to 1885 the outstanding feature of the policy of the Central Authority was the steady pressure exercised through the inspectors with the object of reducing outdoor relief' (1910, p.149). At the same time the overall rate of pauperism declined from 31.2 per 1,000 in 1871-9 to 22.2 per 1,000 in 1896-1905. Thus the nature of poor law relief changed towards institutional care. The workhouse occupied a central position in this system and was ready to welcome the return of the insane. Bearing in mind the character of the workhouse, these figures show that poor relief was becoming increasingly punitive. Whilst it was true that, as Abel-Smith writes, 'few aspects of workhouse life escaped the touch of "less eligibility"' (1964, p.53), workhouse inmates were free to leave if they felt that they could provide for themselves. A circular published in 1871 curtailed this right:

Much evil has arisen and the discipline of the workhouse has been seriously impaired by the frequent power which inmates have hitherto possessed of discharging themselves at short and uncertain notice, claiming readmission as might best suit their inclination and convenience (quoted in Webb and Webb, 1910, p.164).

This situation was altered in the same year by the statute empowering the guardians to detain any workhouse inmate. Thus not only did the workhouse come to occupy a more central position in the relief of poverty, it also became more powerful and controlling. The overflow of the asylum population into the workhouse must be seen as part of the crusade in favour of the workhouse system.

The manifest inadequacies and lack of success of the asylums parallels that of the voluntary hospitals. Both hospitals and lunatic asylums were built as a result of the efforts of philanthropists and both were isolated from and unable to deal with the problems of society. The voluntary hospitals kept their work down to manageable proportions by excluding diseases which they were not able to treat as well as large and undesirable segments of the population (for a fuller discussion of this topic see John Woodward's *To Do the Sick No Harm*, 1974). Thus by a very careful selection of cases admitted the hospitals were able to ensure a degree of success. The asylums, somewhat belatedly, learnt to practise a similar policy. The price at which this qualified success was achieved was isolation from society – the asylum did not serve the society which it had set out to serve.

Henry Maudsley

Resignation and fear had become the pervading attitude to insanity. The outlook of the period is perhaps best reflected in the work of Henry Maudsley. Maudsley was a prolific writer whose books were first published in the early 1870s. His career as a writer is dominated by a few salient themes. One theme is the inexorable force of heredity, another, the powerlessness of outer events to sway a man's genetically determined destiny. For example, he writes:

> But great as is the power of education, it is yet a sternly limited power; it is limited by the power of the individual in nature, and can only work within this larger or smaller circle of necessity, no training in the world will avail to elicit grapes from thorns or figs from thistles; in like manner no mortal can transcend his nature: and it will ever be impossible to raise grapes from thorns or figs from thistles; and it will ever be impossible to raise a stable superstructure of intellect on bad natural foundations (Maudsley, 1874, p.20).

It is an undisputable though extreme fact that certain human
beings are born with such a native deficiency of mind that all
the training and education in the world will not raise them to
the level of brutes; and I believe it to be not less true, that in
consequence of evil ancestral influences, individuals are born
with such a flaw or warp of nature that all care in the world
will not prevent them from being vicious or criminal, or
becoming insane . . . No one can escape the tyranny of his
organization; no one can elude the destiny that is innate in
him, and which unconsciously and irresistibly shapes his ends,
even when he believes that he is determining them with
consummate foresight and skill (1873, p.76).

Maudsley's attitude towards the individual and his powers of self-
improvement are in sharp contrast to the moral managers. His book
Responsibility in Mental Disease (1874) is largely a rebuttal of earlier
writers who had advocated man's power to combat insanity and had
emphasized responsibility for all aberrant conditions. Maudsley,
however, thought that

it would be quite useless to inculcate rules for self-formation
upon one whose character had taken a certain mould of
development; for character is a slow and gradual growth
through action in relation to the circumstances of life; it cannot
be fashioned suddenly and through reflection only. A man can
no more will than he can speak without having learned to do
so, nor can he be taught volition any more than he can be
taught speech except by practice. It was a pregnant saying that
the history of a man is his character; to which one might add
that whatsoever would transform a character must undo a life
history. The fixed and unchanging laws by which events come
to pass hold sway in the mind as in every other domain of
nature (1874, p.272).

This last sentence more than any other sums up Maudsley's
philosophy. Psychological determinism is merely part of a wider
world view which sees the natural and social world as governed by
immutable laws. Character, like social status, is achieved gradually
and not fashioned suddenly overnight. In keeping with this outlook
there is no way of avoiding madness:

Suicide or madness is the natural end of a morbidly sensitive nature, with a feeble will, unable to contend with the hard experience of life. You might as well, in truth, preach moderation to the hurricane as talk philosophy to one whose antecedent life has conducted him to the edge of madness (ibid., p.273).

Character can only be developed very gradually in the same way as a man's social position is gradually gained through hard work and persistent effort. A further quotation is particularly revealing:

It would scarcely be an exaggeration to say that few persons go mad, save from palpable physical causes, who do not show more or less plainly by their gait, manner, gestures, habits of thought, feeling, and action, that they have a sort of predestination to madness. The inherited liability may be strong or weak; it may be so weak as hardly to peril sanity amidst the most adverse circumstances of life, or so strong as to issue in an outbreak of madness – amidst the most favourable external circumstances. Now it is certain that if we were interested in the breeding of a variety of animals, we should not think of breeding from a stock which was wanting in those qualities that were the highest characteristics of the species: we would not willingly select for breeding purposes a hound that was deficient in scent, or a greyhound that was deficient in speed, or a racehorse that could neither stay nor gallop fast. Is it right then to sanction propagation of his kind by an individual who is wanting in that which is the highest attribute of man – a sound and stable mental constitution? (ibid., p.276).

Thus in addition to the inevitability of one's constitution a second theme is introduced which emphasizes the threat which the insane pose for society as a whole. Insanity is no longer seen as a problem to be grappled with by individual will-power, but it has become a major social problem which threatens the health of the nation rather than mere individual autonomy. The insane are thought to constitute a reservoir of bad heredity. Insanity cannot, therefore, be combated by individual moral means. Rather it must be controlled by large-scale biological engineering – in other words, by selective breeding. The hopelessness of the insane means that at most they can be controlled or subjugated by external means but their behaviour cannot be ameliorated by psychological techniques. There is little hope of cure. In fact, the insane and the idiotic are thought to constitute distinct categories, almost a sub-species of humanity. This is thought to be particularly true of idiots: 'In the conformation and habits of other idiots the most careless observer could not help seeing the ape' (Maudsley, 1873, p.48). And Maudsley goes on to cite Pinel's description of one of his idiot patients who resembled

> a sheep in respect of her tastes, her mode of life, and the form of her head. She had an aversion from meat, and ate fruit and vegetables greedily, and drank nothing but water. Her demonstrations of sensibility, joy or trouble, were confined to the repetition of the ill-articulated words be', ma, bah . . . she slept on the floor in the posture of animals (ibid., p.49).

Maudsley describes these animal-like characteristics as marks of extreme human degeneracy or, more precisely, of arrested development:

> When we reflect that every human brain does, in the course of its development, pass through the same stages as the brains of other vertebrate animals, and that its transitional states resemble the permanent forms of their brains; and when we reflect further, that the stages of its development in the womb may be considered the abstract and brief chronicle of a series of developments that have gone through countless ages in nature, it does not seem so wonderful as at first blush it might do, that it should, when in a condition of arrested development, sometimes display animal instinct (ibid., p.52).

Thus psychological morbidity and idiocy are set within a wider evolutionary framework and explained by it. Maudsley's approach to criminals is similar. According to him habitual criminals 'constitute a morbid or degenerate variety of mankind, marked by peculiar low physical and mental characteristics', and there follows a particularly unappetising and detailed description of them. Finally, criminal conduct is explained as follows:

> Their evil propensities are veritable instincts, in spite of reason, and producing when not gratified, a restlessness which becomes at times uncontrollable . . . We may take it then that there is a class of criminals formed of beings of defective physical and mental organization; one result of the defect, which really determines their destiny in life, being an extreme deficiency or

complete absence of moral sense: that an absence of moral sense may be a congenital vice or fault of organization (ibid., pp.128-31).

Thus crime, like insanity, has now become the object of the physician's attention and concern. Moreover, as in the case of the insane, the outlook for the criminal is essentially bleak. Maudsley concurs with a prison surgeon who holds that there is

> a distinct and incurable criminal class, marked by peculiar low physical and mental characteristics; that crime is heredity in the families of criminals belonging to this class; and that this hereditary crime is a disorder of mind, having close relations of nature and descent to epilepsy, dipsomania, insanity and other forms of degeneracy. Such criminals are really morbid varieties, and often exhibit marks of physical degeneration·. ... (ibid., p.66).

The separateness and immutability of the insane, the idiotic and the criminal is emphasized and their distinctiveness explained in terms of native peculiarity or a hereditary neurosis. The differences between individuals are inborn and education can in no way iron them out:

> Multitudes of individuals come into this world weighted with a destiny against which they have neither the will nor the power to contend; they are the step-children of nature and groan under the worst of all tyrannies – the tyranny of a bad organization (ibid., p.43).

The insistence on the existence of morbid or degenerate varieties of mankind is made over and over again in Maudsley's different books. Low intellect and absence of moral sense is paralleled by extreme ugliness and, sometimes, physical deformity. Maudsley is writing about a vast sub-stratum of the English population and ultimately about the dangers of a deterioration of race. Words like species, variety, degeneracy, inheritance and tyranny of organization recur throughout his works.

Furneaux Jordan
Maudsley's work exerted great influence during the late nineteenth century and other writers of the period expressed similar ideas. Another writer whose views are typical of the period is Furneaux

Jordan and his book *Character as seen in Body and Parentage* was published in 1886. In it he reiterates the familiar theme 'that to organization, in other words to inheritance, is mainly due the existence of criminals, paupers, drunkards, lunatics and suicides' (ibid., p.112). Character is seen as limiting a person's possible achievements, not as something which may be altered and bettered during a lifetime by individual effort. Ideas about the individual have become doom-laden and his powers are seen as being extremely restricted. The use of the word 'inheritance' as a synonym for heredity is particularly interesting given the two meanings which it has. One meaning is that of becoming heir to property and the other refers to biological endowment. The use of such a term suggests that the two ideas of biological and social endowment were closely linked in the minds of late Victorian physicians: those who were socially well endowed were also likely to be thought biologically superior. Degenerate stock was by and large confined to the pauper or disreputable classes. With the huge expansion of asylums described earlier, the problem had become one of large masses of population. These changes in attitude to insanity conform with the historian, Dicey's categorization of the nineteenth century. Dicey describes the period until 1830 as one of Tory paternalism, the period between 1830 and 1865 is characterized as one of utilitarian reform, and the period thereafter is characterized as one of collectivism and wholesale intervention (1962). With respect to attitudes to the insane, this characterization of the century certainly fits. The very size of the problem had forced a collective attitude towards and collective solutions of lunacy.

General paralysis of the insane

However, quite apart from the increasing size of the problem and the new emphasis on race, its degeneracy and moral deterioration, the increasing incidence of syphilis and general paralysis in insane asylums must have influenced ideas about insanity. E.H. Hare, in a carefully written paper called 'The Origin and Spread of Dementia Paralytica' (1959) argues that 'dementia paralytica from being a rare disease or even non-existent, suddenly assumed epidemic prevalence in Northern France soon after the Napoleonic Wars' (ibid., p.595). In France the disease was first described by Esquirol in the second decade of the nineteenth century. Before that time there were no descriptions of the condition which might have been general paralysis of the insane: 'This failure to describe dementia paralytica would – if the disease had been there to describe – be all the more surprising when we take into account the striking clinical syndrome which it commonly presented' (ibid., p.604). One of the first English physicians to make mention of it is Conolly (1849, p.39) followed by Bucknill (1857) and Maudsley, who writes: 'The group of cases described under this head (general paralysis) unquestionably constitute the most definite and satisfactory example of a clinical variety of a mental disease' (1879, p.432). Thus clear and easily recognizable descriptions of general paralysis appeared in the course of the century. James Cowles Prichard writing in 1833 found little evidence of general paralysis. By 1849 John Conolly found it to be common in all the asylums of England. Throughout the latter half of the century the disease increased.

By the beginning of the twentieth century the Commissioners in Lunacy reported that between the years 1901 and 1911 postmortem examinations revealed that over 70 per cent of asylum patients were suffering from general paralysis. Hare writes that 'Towards the end of the nineteenth century the association between syphilis and dementia paralytica became increasingly well esablished' (1959, p.614), so much so that Krafft-Ebing could coin the aphorism 'civilization and syphilization'. During the twentieth century, however, before the advent of effective treatment, the incidence of syphilis declined. What is certain is that the wide incidence of syphilis and its neat explanatory powers offered a tempting model to which other explanations of insanity might aspire. In a recent article in the *British Journal of Psychiatry* (1976, 129, pp.308-16) Szasz argues that the investigation of neurosyphilis played a decisive though totally misleading part in the development of psychiatry. Schizophrenia, in particular, has suffered from being subsumed under the paradigm of syphilis. This paradigm has encouraged the illegitimate translation of histopathology to psychopathology and has led to the 'greatest epistemological translation of our medical age'. This is yet another illustration of Szasz's argument – that the supposedly clear model of disease as physical lesion cannot be transferred to mental illness. There is much historical material to explain why the paradigm of syphilis should have achieved such dominance and Szasz cites hospital statistics from the early part of this century to show that between 20 and 30 per cent of psychiatric patients were suffering from syphilitic paralysis. The figures which Hare gives are much higher, but whatever the precise figures were it is clear that the influence of general paralysis on psychiatric explanations was large (Hare, 1959). However, there were other factors which contributed towards the pessimistic outlook in psychiatry and the dominance of biological explanations of insanity. These relate to difficulties encountered within asylums and their inability to grapple with the social and psychological problems with which they were presented.

The insane in America
By the late nineteenth century the asylum system had reached its full flowering. Emphasis was put on insanity as a disease with a physical cause, albeit unspecified. Rothman in his book *The Discovery of the Asylum* (1971) argues that in America at least the asylum came to represent order and stability in the midst of change; the very symmetry of the buildings reflected its ideals of orderliness. However, the asylum contained the seeds of its own destruction precisely because treatment was asylum-based: 'The organizing concepts of the asylum disguised and even subtly encouraged a custodial operation' (ibid., p.270). During the era of moral management care of the insane took place in small family-like units. As the asylum grew in size such individual attention was no longer possible and, with increasing numbers, the old methods of physical restraint and regimentation returned. The collective treatment of the insane became a necessity with the increasing size of the insane population.

The process which Rothman describes as taking place in America is very like that which took place in English asylums. A fluid society promoted faith in the possibility of a cure of insanity within the asylum. In both England and America emphasis was put upon order and regularity within the asylum. Rothman writes: 'Thus the insane asylum, like other corrective institutions, in the Jacksonian period, represented both an attempt to compensate for public disorder in a particular setting and to demonstrate the correct rules of social organization' (1971, p.154). However, within a short space of time the asylums had changed from small family-like units to vast hopeless units. Despite this transformation and obvious lack of success the asylum continued to grow. It became the refuge of a heterogeneous mass of people, including, in America, large numbers of immigrants. They were no longer classified, pretence to cure was abandoned and physical restraint was introduced. Thus the development of the asylum in England and America had much in common.

9
Conclusion

This historical study has been encouraged by the following view of psychiatric ideas and practice. Namely, that psychiatry is permeated with social values and, therefore, that its changes throughout history are, at least partly, related to changing values.

Diagnoses of mental disorder have been and are made because behaviour or mood is disturbed. Human behaviour only makes sense in the light of the values and rules by which it is governed and inevitably, therefore, what counts as disorder will depend upon the ideals of behaviour at any one period. From this it does not follow that what is called mental illness is totally arbitrary and subject to infinite variations according to the values of a society. It may well be that some forms of behaviour contravene the expected standards of all societies - for example extreme withdrawal and indiscriminate violence may be instances of such unacceptable behaviour. Nevertheless, the initial identification of a particular piece of behaviour as a medical problem and the subsequent search for an organic basis to the disturbance has been largely guided by the moral tenor of the age. The examples in this book have provided illustrations of this point. Frequently the fashions in psychiatric diagnoses provide a clue to the personality characteristics most highly valued; the description of an illness often incorporates characteristics opposite to those of the ideal human being or a caricature of them. For example, the masturbator whose vice leads to insanity epitomizes loss of the most highly valued human attribute - self-control; excess of imagination is thought to constitute insanity at a time when reasonableness was highly valued.

In a recently published book *Reasoning about Madness* (1978) the psychiatrist John Wing suggests that the term 'illness' can be used in two ways. In the first, it refers to 'any experience or behaviour which departs from a generally accepted standard of health', in its second use to 'a limited and relatively specific theory is put forward because it is thought to be relevant to the reduction of some recognizable impairment. The term madness should be used in the first of these two ways' (ibid., p.141). Wing argues that psychiatrists should properly be concerned with illness in a technically specific sense dealing with impairment. He thinks that the group of functional illnesses will diminish as psychiatry progresses. In his view the realm of illness dealt with by the psychiatrist is completely distinct from lay conceptions of madness and mental disorder; the layman's conception of madness and the diagnoses made by the psychiatrist refer to different kinds of phenomena and although the two conceptions may on occasion overlap they need not do so. In order to lend weight to this dichotomous approach Wing refers to Locke's distinction between two kinds of madness: the first madness involves opposition to reason, the second involves being overpowered by unruly passions. Wing takes Locke's distinction as being the equivalent of the contemporary distinction between unreasonableness or eccentricity, and illness. Psychiatrists should restrict themselves to dealing with the basic core of mental illness, to Locke's use of madness as the equivalent of engulfment by unruly passions. This is the legitimate realm of activity of psychiatrists and if they confine themselves to it they are practising clinical science. However, the distinction between the two types of madness should remain clear according to Wing.

Wing is claiming that although social factors may influence minor and trivial psychiatric disorders, namely those at the bottom of the hierarchy of psychiatric disorders, there is nevertheless an irreducible residuum of psychiatric disorder which remains constant over time and place and which is only influenced in certain minor and relatively insignificant ways by social factors. Leaving to one side the issue of whether the distinction exists and whether it is as clear cut and irreconcilable as Wing claims, it is quite evident that this book has dealt with common conceptions of madness which Wing claims are not the legitimate province of the contemporary psychiatrist. In earlier periods these common conceptions of madness were put forward by doctors and the contemporary rift between lay and professional views had not yet taken place. For example, Wing claims that the terms psychosis and neurosis are not really the concern of psychiatrists:

> Like many psychiatric terms derived from Greek roots they promise a technical specificity that should clear up the confusion of terms like 'madness' and 'neurosis'. In fact, countless inconclusive battles have been fought over the implications of each one during the course of a century or more, and without further specification the meaning is still not clear (ibid., p.44).

Psychiatry should be concerned only with those disorders for which there are precise criteria of recognition.

Whatever the present goals of Wing and other psychiatrists, it is clear that psychiatry in the past has not achieved this degree of precision and that it has dealt with matters which Wing would claim are not its legitimate concern. Whilst this may have detracted from the scientific precision of psychiatry, it has nevertheless added interest to its history. All we have are written records of behaviour and we can never check these against reality. A historical study is, therefore, inevitably restricted to illness in the first sense, that is, a departure from some expected standard of health. The actual impairment has long since disappeared and we have few means of reconstructing it or measuring its severity. Whatever the goals of present day psychiatrists in terms of conforming to stringent rules of scientific method, the sociologist or historian is more interested in actual practice which so often falls short of the high ideals which the psychiatrist has set himself. This does not necessarily mean that the historian or sociologist thinks that the rules of scientific method are inapplicable, merely that they have not always been successfully applied. History does not tell us how psychiatry should be practised, only how it has been practised. The permeation of medicine and psychiatry by social values and norms is not an argument for the take-over of psychiatry by the social sciences, it is not an argument for sociological expansion or imperialism with regard to *psychiatric practice,* but it is an argument for the need of a sociological dimension to the *study of psychiatric practice.*

Anthony Clare in his book *Psychiatry in Dissent* (1976) has put forward a defence of the medical model in psychiatry. He argues that despite the seeming ideological confusion in psychiatry at present, the medical model is able to encompass within itself social, psychological and biological dimensions.

It is often erroneously believed that this model (i.e. the medical) and the 'organic' orientation, which stresses a physical basis for psychiatric illness to the exclusion of other factors, are synonymous. The medical model is an evolving one in which scientific methods of observation, description, and differentiation are employed, in which an illness is conceptualized as a 'process that moves from the recognition and palliation of symptoms to the characterization of a specific disease in which the etiology and pathogenesis are known and the treatment is rational and specific'. Such a process may take years, centuries even, and while many medical conditions have moved to the final stages of such understanding, others are still at various points along the way (Clare, 1976, p.68).

From the point of view of contemporary critics of psychiatry Clare lays himself open to attack. If the medical model is indeed, as he describes, a perpetually evolving model, then it is a moving target, forever eluding criticism. Although this position does not enhance the theoretical standing of the medical model, it does support a historical review of the practice of psychiatry.

Peter Sedgwick in an important but little known article called 'Mental Illness is Illness' (1972) argues, as the title suggests, against the separation of mental from physical illness. His argument is not the common one that mental illness has an organic component if not an organic basis, but rather that the recognition of any illness necessarily involves value judgments. For example, 'The blight that strikes at corn or at potatoes is a human invention, for if men wished to cultivate parasites (rather than potatoes or corn) there would be no "blight", but simply the necessary foddering of the parasite-crop' (ibid., p.211). Sedgwick gives another striking example: 'The fracture of a septuagenarian's femur has, within the world of nature, no more significance than the snapping of an autumn leaf from its twig' (ibid., p.211). Illnesses are bestowed upon nature by man, in cases where failure would affect his well-being. This infiltration of the physical world by values provides yet another invitation to the social scientist to explore medical history.

An awareness of such theoretical issues has been partly responsible for directing my interest towards the history of psychiatry. So too has my somewhat anomalous position as a social anthropologist within a clinical department of mental health which has encouraged me to adopt a more detached and relativist perspective on psychiatric beliefs and practices.

As a final task my indebtedness to the writing of George Rosen and his influence on my work need to be recorded. Rosen's work reflects immense learning and he delights the reader by unearthing forgotten episodes of medical history. A recently published example is his account of *nostalgia,* a disease suffered by soldiers away from home (Rosen, 1975). However, his importance lies in the way in which he situates medical ideas. He contrasts his approach with the iatrocentric approach which is dominant in the writing of medical history:

> In fact, the iatrocentric approach has characterized the work of most medical historians and is still prominent among us. Nor is it surprising that this is so for until very recently those who wrote on medical history were almost without exception themselves physicians, and in many instances physicians who were or had been in some form of practice. For historians whose view of medicine was determined largely by the frame of reference of the medical profession, it seemed perfectly natural to regard the scope of medical history as bounded by those aspects with which their own interests and sentiments are identified. Furthermore, the concept of the autonomous character of medical history was reinforced by viewing the history of medicine as a fairly steady progression from darkness to light through scientific discovery and technical innovation (Rosen, 1967a, p.8).

Rosen, by contrast, suggests that medical history should be social history and that equal attention should be paid to the patient as to the doctor:

> Thus to view health and its problems within a societal context rather than as defined by the professional interests of physicians, it becomes necessary to learn about people with whom the healers at any given period are concerned. This involves the ascertainment as far as feasible, of population structure and change, modes of life, occupations, social organization, including such matters as the social position of women,

children, old people and other social groups whose place in the social system may have an influence on their health (ibid., p.10).

To the social scientist the claim that psychiatric history should be social history seems obvious; to others it may need some explanation. The development of ideas about madness seldom unfolds in simple linear order. Psychiatric ideas cannot be understood solely in terms of their development from earlier ideas or in terms of the way in which they relate to other scientific ideas of the time. Psychiatry deals with people and it is, therefore, inevitably influenced by the values, beliefs and attitudes important at a particular period. Thus the investigation of ideas about madness is no longer a straightforward historical narrative but acquires a socio-historical dimension. As an ideal this is highly commendable, in practice it may not be possible to document all aspects of society. Nevertheless, the goals are worth pursuing.

Perhaps I should add that in writing this book I have set myself modest goals. I have not tried to provide a complete history of madness although I hope a certain sense of historical narrative has been achieved. Neither have I tried to present a sustained argument in defence of a theoretical position. Given the present state of knowledge of the history of madness I feel that this might have been premature. Rather, I have tried to communicate the intrinsic interest of a relatively unknown area when viewed from a socio-historical perspective. If I am criticized for not providing that perspective very fully, then I can only reply that I hope this book will encourage others to do so better.

Some Important Dates

1774 Act for the regulation of private madhouses with a seven mile radius of London passed (14 Geo.III, c.49)

1792 Retreat for the Quaker insane founded at York by William Tuke

1782-1820 Reign of George III who suffered from several distinct and prolonged episodes of what was thought to be insanity

1805 Parliamentary Select Committee set up to inquire into condition of criminal and pauper lunatics

1806 Act passed recommending that each county build an asylum for the care of its insane

1806 First English translation of Pinel's *Traité de l'Aliénation*

1813 *A Description of the Retreat* by Samuel Tuke published

1815 Select Committee set up to investigate the scandalous conditions of lunatics. William Norris discovered chained by the neck in Bethlem

1827 Select Committee appointed to inquire into the condition of metropolitan madhouses

1833 James Cowles Prichard published *A Treatise on Insanity* in which moral insanity is first identified

1839 *Total Abolition of Personal Restraint* by Robert Gardiner Hill published

1841 Association of Medical Officers of Asylums and Hospitals for the insane founded. (In 1865 this became the Medico-psychological Association)

1844 Report of the Metropolitan Commissioners which gave details of all aspects of asylum care

1845 Lunatics Act made building of county asylums obligatory

1853 *Asyl: m Journal* first published

1858 Became known as *Journal of Mental Science*

1856 *The Treatment of the Insane without Mechanical Restraints* by John Conolly published

1877 Select Committee set up to inquire into whether the workings of Lunacy Law infringe personal liberty

1890 Lunacy Act formalized the processes of admission to an asylum in order to safeguard against illegal confinement

Bibliography

Abel-Smith, Brian (1964), *The Hospitals,* London, Heinemann.

Acton, William (1857), *Prostitution considered in its moral, social and sanitary aspects,* London, John Churchill & Son.

Acton, William (1865), *The Functions and Disorders of the Reproductive Organs,* London, John Churchill & Son. 4th edn.

Alexander, Franz G., and Seleznick, Sheldon T. (1967), *The History of Psychiatry: An Evaluation of Psychiatric Thought and Practice from Prehistoric Times to the Present,* London, Allen & Unwin.

Allen, Don Cameron (1938), 'The degeneration of man and renaissance pessimism', *Studies in Philology,* vol. 35.

Allen, Matthew (1831), *Essays on the Classification of the Insane.*

Allnatt, R. H. (1843), 'Case of Atrophy of the Testicle from Excessive Masturbation', *Lancet,* ii, pp. 654-5.

Anon. (1710), *Onania, or the Heinous Sin of Self-Pollution and all its Frightful Consequences in Both Sexes,* London.

Anon. (1750), *A Treatise on the Dismal Effects of Low-Spiritedness.*

Anon. (1849), *Confessions of a Hypochondriac or the Adventures of a Hypochondriac in Search of Health,* London, Saunders & Otley.

Arbuthnot, John (1756), *An Essay concerning the nature of Ailments, . . .* to which are added practical rules of diet, London, Tonson.

Ariès, Philippe (1960), *Centuries of Childhood,* Harmondsworth, Penguin.

Aristotle (1927), *The Works of Aristotle Translated into English,* vol. 7, *Problemata,* Oxford, Clarendon Press.

Aubrey, John (1950), *Brief Lives,* ed. Lawson Dick, London, Secker & Secker.

Babb, L. (1951), *The Elizabethan Malady: A Study of Melancholia in English Literature from 1580 to 1640,* East Lansing, Michigan State College Press.

Babb, L. (1959), *Sanity in Bedlam: A Study of Robert Burton's Anatomy of Melancholy,* East Lansing, Michigan State University.

Banks, J. A. (1954), *Prosperity and Parenthood,* London, Routledge & Kegan Paul.

Banks, J. A. and Banks, Olive (1964), *Feminism and Family Planning,* Liverpool University Press.

Barlow, John (1843), *Man's Power over Himself to Prevent or Control Insanity,* London, William Pickering.

Bateson, Gregory (ed.) (1962), *Perceval's Narrative: A Patient's Account of his Psychosis 1830-2,* London, Hogarth Press.

Beck, Ann (1956), 'The British Medical Council and British Medical Education in the Nineteenth Century', *Bulletin of the History of Medicine,* vol. 30, pp. 154-61.

Bell, Charles (1806), *The Anatomy of Expression,* London, John Murray, 3rd edn., 1844

Best, Geoffrey (1964), *Shaftesbury,* London, Batsford.

Blackmore, Richard (1725), *A Treatise of the Spleen and Vapours: or, Hypochondriacal and Hysterical Affections,* London, J. Pemberton.

Bloch, Marc (1973), *The Royal Touch: Sacred Monarchy and Scrofula in England and France,* London, Routledge & Kegan Paul and McGill, Queens University Press.

Boswell, James (1951), *Boswell's Column,* being his seventy contributions to the London Magazine under the pseudonym 'The Hypochondriack' from 1778 to 1783. Introd. and notes by Margery Bailey, London, Kimber.

Boswell, James (1961), *Journal of a Tour to the Hebrides with Samuel Johnson,* ed. R. W. Chapman.

Boucherett, Jessie (1869), 'How to provide for superfluous women', *Woman's Work and Woman's Culture,* ed. Josephine Butler, pp. 27-48, London, Macmillan.

Branca, Patricia (1975), *Silent Sisterhood. Middle Class Women in the Victorian Home,* London, Croom Helm.

Brand, Jeanne L. (1961), 'The Parish Doctor: England's Poor Law Medical Officers and Medical Reform, 1870-1900', *Bulletin of the History of Medicine,* vol. 35, no. 2, pp. 97-122.

Breton, Nicholas (1929), *Melancholike Humours.* London, The Scholartis Press (first published 1600). Edited with an Essay on Elizabethan Melancholy by G. B. Harrison pp. 49-89.

Bright, Timothy (1586), *A Treatise of Melancholy,* London, Thomas Vautrolier.

Brown, John (1757), *Estimate of the Manners and Principles of the Times,* London, L. Davis & C. Reymers. 2nd edn.

Browne, Richard (1729), *Medicina Musica, to which is annexed a new essay on the Nature and Cure of the Spleen and Vapours,* London.

Bucknill, Charles (1854), *Unsoundness of Mind in Relation to Criminal Insanity,* London, Longman, Brown, Green & Longmans.

Bucknill, Charles (1857), 'The Diagnosis of Insanity', *Journal of Mental Science,* vol. 3, p. 141.

Bullough, Vera and Voght, Martha (1973), 'Women, Menstruation and Nineteenth Century Medicine', *Bulletin of the History of Medicine,* no. 47, pp. 66-82.

Burgess, Thomas (1828), *The Physiology or Mechanism of Blushing,* London, John Churchill.

Burrow, J. W. (1966), *Evolution and Society*, Cambridge University Press.

Burrows, George Man (1828), *Commentaries on Insanity*, London, Underwood.

Burton, Robert (1621), *The Anatomy of Melancholy*, London, J. E. Hodson, 11th edn., 1806.

Bynum, W. F. (1974), 'Rationales for Therapy in British Psychiatry 1780-1834', *Medical History*, vol. 18 pp. 317-34.

Byrd, Max (1974), *Visits to Bedlam*, Columbia, University of South Carolina Press.

Campbell, Archibald (1730), *A Discourse proving that the Apostles were no Enthusiasts*, London, A. Millar.

Caplan, Ruth (1969), *Psychiatry and the Community in Nineteenth Century America*, New York, Basic Books.

Carlson, E. T. and Dain, N. (1962), 'The meaning of moral insanity', *Bulletin of the History of Medicine*, vol. 36, pp. 130-40.

Carlson, Eric T. and Simpson, Merideth M. (1969), 'Madness of the Nervous System in Eighteenth Century Psychiatry', *Bulletin of the History of Psychiatry*, vol. 43, pp. 101-15.

Carter, Robert B. (1853), *On the Pathology and Treatment of Hysteria*, London.

Casaubon, Meric (1655), *A Treatise concerning Enthusiasm, as it is an effect of nature: But is mistaken by many for either divine inspiration, or diabolical possession*, London.

Charron, Pierre (1601), *Of Wisdome Three Bookes*, trans. Samson Lennard, London, c. 1606; later edns. 1630, 1640.

Cheyne, George (1724), *An Essay of Health and Long Life*, London, Strahan & Leake.

Cheyne, George (1734), *The English Malady or a Treatise on Nervous Diseases of all kinds*, London, Strahan & Leake.

Clare, A. (1976), *Psychiatry in Dissent*, London, Tavistock Publications.

Clark, Alice (1919), *The Working Life of Women in the 17th Century*. London, George Routledge & Sons Ltd.

Clarke, Edward H. (1874), *Sex in Education: or a Fair Chance for Girls*, Boston, James R. Osgood & Co.

Clouston, T. S. (1906), *Hygiene of the Mind*, London, Methuen.

Cobbe, Frances Power (1863), 'What shall we do with our old maids?', pp. 58-101, *Essays on the Pursuits of Women*, London, Emily Faithfull.

Colp, Ralph J. M. D. (1977), *To be an Invalid, The Illness of Charles Darwin*, University of Chicago Press.

Comfort, Alex (1967), *The Anxiety Makers*, London, Panther edn. 1968.

Cominos, Peter T. (1965), 'Late Victorian Sexual Respectability and the Social System', *International Review of Social History*, 1965, pp. 18-48, 216-50.

Conolly, John (1849), *On Some Forms of Insanity*, London.

Conolly, John (1856), *The Treatment of the Insane without Mechanical Restraints*, London, Smith Elder & Co.

Coveney, Peter (1951), *The Image of Childhood*, Harmondsworth, Penguin.

Cowen, David L. (1969), 'Liberty, Laissez-Faire and Licensure in Nineteenth

Century Britain', *Bulletin of the History of Medicine,* vol. 43, pp. 30-40.

Cowper, William (1845), *Economy for the single and married by one who makes ends meet,* London.

Crow, Duncan (1971), *The Victorian Woman,* London, Allen & Unwin.

Cunnington, C. Willett (1935), *Feminine Attitudes in the Nineteenth Century,* Heinemann, London.

Curling, T. B. (1856), *A Practical Treatise on Diseases of the Testis,* London, John Churchill.

Dain, Norman (1964), *Concepts of Insanity 1789-1865,* New Brunswick, Rutgers.

Darwin, Charles (1872), *The Expression of Emotion in Man and the Animals,* London, John Murray.

Dawson, Richard (1840), *An Essay on Spermatorrhoea,* London, Aylott Jones. 6th edn., 1852.

Defoe, Daniel (1706), *A Review of the State of the English Nation.*

DePorte, Michael (1974), *Nightmares and Hobby Horses. Swift, Sterne and Augustan ideas of Madness,* San Marino, The Huntington Library.

Dicey, A. V. (1962), *Introduction to the Study of the Law of the Constitution,* London, Macmillan. First published 1912.

Donnison, Jean (1977), *Midwives and Medical Men: A History of Inter-Professional Rivalries and Women's Rights,* London, Heinemann.

Doughty, Oswald (1926), 'The English Malady of the Eighteenth Century', *Review of English Studies,* vol. 11, no. 7, pp. 251-69.

Dover, Thomas (1732), *The Ancient Physician's Legacy to his Country,* London, Bettesworth.

Draper, John W. (1945), *The Humors and Shakespeare's Characters,* Durham, North Carolina, Duke University Press.

Ellis, William Charles (1838), *A Treatise on the Nature, Symptoms, Causes and Treatment of Insanity,* London, Samuel Holdsworth.

Engelhardt, H. Tristram Jr (1971), 'The Disease of Masturbation: Values and the Concept of Disease', *Bulletin of the History of Medicine,* vol. 45, pp. 234-48.

Evans, Berger (1972), *The Psychiatry of Robert Burton,* New York, Octagon Books. First published 1944.

Fischer-Homberger, Esther (1972), 'Hypochondriasis of the Eighteenth Century – Neurosis of the Present Century', *Bulletin of the History of Medicine,* vol. 46, pp. 391-401.

Foucault, Michel (1971), *Madness and Civilization,* London, Tavistock Publications.

Fowler, Robert (1871), *A Complete History of the case of the Welsh fasting girl (Sarah Jacob) with Comments Thereon; and Observations on Death from starvation,* London, Henry Renshaw.

Fox, Arthur W. (1899), *A Book of Bachelors,* London, Constable, pp. 398-436.

Grange, Kathleen (1961), 'Pinel and Eighteenth Century Psychiatry', *Bulletin of the History of Medicine,* vol. 35, pp. 442-53.

Grange, Kathleen (1962), 'The Ship Symbol as a Key to Former Theories of the Emotions', *Bulletin of the History of Medicine,* vol. 36, pp. 512-23.

Greg, W. R. (1877), 'Why are women redundant?', pp. 44-90. *Literary and Social Judgements,* vol. 2, London, Trench, Trubner.

Habakkuk, K. J. (1950), 'Marriage Settlements in the Eighteenth Century', *Transactions of the Royal Historical Society,* vol. 32, 4th series, pp. 15-30.

Haller, John S. and Haller, Robin M. (1974), *The Physician and Sexuality in Victorian America,* Urbana, University of Illinois Press.

Hare, E. H. (1959), 'The Origin and Spread of Dementia Paralytica', *Journal of Mental Science,* vol. 105, pp. 594-626.

Hare, E. H. (1962), 'Masturbational Insanity: the History of an Idea', *Journal of Mental Science,* vol. 108, pp. 1-25.

Hartley, David (1801), *Observations on Man, his frame, his duty and his expectations,* London, Richardson. First published 1749.

Haslam, John (1817), *Considerations on the moral managements of insane persons,* London, R. Hunter.

Harvey, William (1673), *An Anatomical disquisition on the motion of the heart and blood in animals,* trans. from Latin by Robert Williams, London, Dent, 1907.

Hill, A. W. (1958), *John Wesley among the Physicians: a study of Eighteenth Century medicine,* London, Epworth Press.

Hill, Christopher (1956), 'Clarissa Harlow and her Times', in *Puritanism and Revolution,* London, Panther edn. (1968), pp. 351-76.

Hill, Robert Gardiner (1839), *Total Abolition of Personal Restraint in the Treatment of the Insane,* London, Simpkin & Marshall.

Himes, Norman (1936), *Medical History of Contraception,* London, Allen & Unwin.

Hobbes, Thomas (1962), *Leviathan,* London, Fontana. First edition 1651.

Hodder, Edwin (1886), *The Life and Work of the Seventh Earl of Shaftesbury,* in 3 vols., London, Cassell.

Hodgkinson, Ruth G. (1966), 'Provision for Pauper Lunatics 1834-1871', *Medical History,* vol. 10, pp. 138-54.

Hodgkinson, Ruth G. (1967), *The Origins of the National Health Service,* London, Wellcome Historical Medical Library.

Hoeldtke, Robert (1967), 'The History of Associationism', *Medical History,* vol. 11, pp. 46-65.

Howells, John G. (ed.) (1975), *World History of Psychiatry,* London, Baillière Tindall.

Hudson, Derek (1972), *Munby, Man of Two Worlds: The Life and Diaries of Arthur J. Munby 1828-1910,* John Murray.

Hume, David (1734), *Letters of David Hume,* ed. J. Y. T. Greig, Oxford University Press, 1932 edn.

Hunter, Richard and Macalpine, Ida (1962), 'John Thomas Perceval (1803-1876) Patient and Reformer', *Medical History,* vol. 6, pp. 391-5.

Hunter, Richard and Macalpine, Ida (1963), *Three Hundred Years of Psychiatry 1535-1860: A History Presented in Selected English Texts,* London, Oxford University Press.

Hunter, Richard and Macalpine, Ida (1969), *George III and the Mad Business,* London, Allen Lane.

Hunter, Richard and Macalpine, Ida (1974), *Psychiatry for the Poor: Colney Hatch Asylum-Hospital. A Medical and Social History,* London, Dawsons.

Hutchinson, Francis (1708), *A Short view of the Pretended Spirit of Prophecy, taken from its first rise in the year 1688 to its present state among us,* London, J. Morphew.

Johnson, Samuel (1958), *Diaries, Prayers and Annals,* ed. E. L. McAdam Jr with Donald and Mary Hyde, New Haven.

Johnson, Samuel (1976), *Johnson on Johnson,* ed. J. Wain, London, Dent.

Jones, Kathleen (1972), *A History of the Mental Health Services,* London, Routledge & Kegan Paul.

Jordan, Furneaux (1886), *Character as Seen in Body and Parentage,* London, Kegan Paul, Trench, Trubner.

Jorden, Edward (1603), *A Briefe Discourse of a Disease called Suffocation of the Mother,* London.

Kavka, Jerome (1949), 'Pinel's Conception of the Psychopathic State', *Bulletin of the History of Medicine,* vol. 23, pp. 461-8.

Knights, L. C. (1937), *Drama and Society in the Age of Jonson,* London, Chatto & Windus. (Appendix B 'Seventeenth Century Melancholy', pp. 315-32.)

Lallemand, J. (1847), *A Treatise on Spermatorrhoea,* trans. Henry J. McDougall, London, John Churchill.

Lavater, Johann Caspar (1778), *Essays on Physiognomy,* London, William Tegg & Co. 5th edn., 1848.

Laycock, Thomas (1840), *A Treatise on Nervous Diseases of Women,* London, Longman, Orme, Brown, Green & Longmans.

Lewis, Aubrey (1951), 'Henry Maudsley: his Work and Influence', *Journal of Mental Science,* vol. 97, pp. 159-277.

Lewis, Aubrey (1955), 'Philippe Pinel and the English', *Proceedings of the Royal Society of Medicine,* vol. 48, pp. 581-6.

Lichtenberg, Georg (1783), 'Fragment von Schwanzen', *Baldingers Neues Magazin für Ärzte,* 5.

Locke, John (1959), *An Essay concerning Human Understanding,* London, Dover. First published 1690.

Lucas, E. V. (1905), *The Works of Charles and Mary Lamb,* Oxford University Press.

Lyons, B. G. (1971), *Voices of Melancholy: Studies in Literary Treatments of Melancholy in Renaissance England,* London, Routledge & Kegan Paul.

Macalpine, Ida and Hunter, Richard (1956), *Schizophrenia 1677,* A psychiatric study of an illustrated autobiographical record of demoniacal possession, London, W. Dawson.

McGregor, O. R. (1955), 'The Social Position of Women in England 1850-1914: A Bibliography', *British Journal of Sociology,* pp. 48-60.

Maddock, Alfred Beaumont (1854), *Practical Observations on Mental and Nervous Disorders,* London, Simpkin, Marshall & Co.

Mandeville, Bernard de (1711), *A Treatise of the Hypochondriack and Hysterick Passions,* London, Tonson.

Mandeville, Bernard de (1724), *Poem of the Fable of the Bees: A Modest Defence of Public Stews,* Augustan Reprint Society Publication 162.

Marcus, Steven (1969), *The Other Victorians,* London, Corgi, Weidenfeld & Nicolson (1966).

Martineau, Harriet (1859), 'Female Industry', *Edinburgh Review,* vol. 222, pp. 293-336.

Maturin, Charles (1968), *Melmoth the Wanderer: a Tale,* ed. Douglas Grant, Oxford University Press. First published 1820.

Maudsley, Henry (1868), 'Illustrations of a Variety of Insanity', *Journal of Mental Science,* 14, pp. 149-62.

Maudsley, Henry (1873), *Body and Mind,* London, Macmillan.

Maudsley, Henry (1874), *Responsibility in Mental Disease,* London, Henry S. King & Co.

Maudsley, Henry (1874), 'Sex in Mind and in Education', *Fortnightly Review,* vol. 21, pp. 466-83.

Maudsley, Henry (1879), *The Pathology of Mind,* London, Macmillan.

Maudsley, Henry (1886), *Natural Causes and Supernatural Seemings,* London, Kegan Paul, Trench, Trubner & Co.

Milton, John (1854), 'On the Nature and Treatment of Spermatorrhoea', *Lancet,* 1, pp. 243-6, 269-70, 467-8, 595-6.

Milton, John (1887), *Pathology and Treatment of Spermatorrhoea,* London, Henry Renshaw.

Mitford, John (1823), *A Description of the Crimes and Horrors in the interior of Warburton's private madhouse at Hoxton,* London, Belfour.

Moore, C. A. (1953), 'The English Malady', in *Backgrounds of English Literature 1700-60,* Minneapolis, University of Minnesota Press.

Mora, George and Brand, Jeanne L. (eds) (1970), *Psychiatry and its History: Methodological Problems in Research,* Illinois, Charles C. Thomas.

Morison, Alexander (1824), *Outlines of Mental Diseases,* Edinburgh, McLachlan & Stewart.

Mornay, Philippe de (1602), *True Knowledge of Man's Owne Selfe,* trans. Anthony Munday, London.

Mueller, William R. (1952), *The Anatomy of Robert Burton's England,* Berkeley and Los Angeles, University of California Press.

Mullett, Charles F. (1951), 'The Lay Outlook on Medicine in England, Circa 1800-1850', *Bulletin of the History of Medicine,* vol. 25, pp. 169-77.

Musher, Daniel M. (1967), 'The Medical Views of Dr. Tobias Smollett 1721-1771', *Bulletin of the History of Medicine,* 41, pp. 455-62.

Needham, Gwendolyn Bridges and Utter, Robert Palfrey (1937), 'Liquid Sorrow' in *Pamela's Daughters,* London, Lovat Dickson.

Noble, Daniel (1853), *Elements of Psychological Medicine,* London, John Churchill.

Olivier, Edith (1934), *The Eccentric Life of Alexander Cruden,* London, Faber & Faber.

Osler, Sir William (1914), 'Burton's Anatomy of Melancholy', *Yale Review,* New Series, III, pp. 251-71.

Parry-Jones, William (1972), *The Trade in Lunacy. A Study of Private Madhouses in England in the Eighteenth and Nineteenth Centuries,* London, Routledge & Kegan Paul.

Parsons, Ralph W. (1907), 'The American Girl *versus* higher education, considered from a medical point of view', *New York Medical Journal,* 85, p.116.

Paternoster, Richard (1841), *The Madhouse System.*

Peers, Edgar Allison (1914), *Elizabethan Drama and its Mad Folk,* Cambridge, Heffer.

Perceval, John (1838), *Perceval's Narrative.*

Philipps, M. and Tomkinson, W. S. (1926), *English Women in Life and Letters,* Oxford University Press.

Pinel, Philippe (1806), *A Treatise on Insanity, in which are contained the principles of nosology of maniacal disorders,* trans. D. D. Davis, Sheffield, Todd.

Prichard, James Cowles (1833), *A Treatise on Insanity,* London, Marchant.

Purcell, John (1702), *A Treatise of Vapours and Hysteric Fits,* London, E. Place.

Reade, Charles (1898), *Hard Cash. A Matter of Fact Romance,* London, Chatto & Windus. First published 1863.

Reynolds, Edward (1640), *A Treatise of the Passions and Faculties of the Soule of Man,* London.

Robin, P. A. (1911), *The Old Physiology in English Literature,* London, J. M. Dent.

Robinson, Nicholas (1729), *A New System of the Spleen, Vapours and Hypochondriack Melancholy,* London, Bettesworth.

Rogers, Thomas (1576), *Anatomie of the Minde: A Philosophical Discourse Entitled The Anatomie of the Minde,* London.

Rosen, George (1951), 'Romantic Medicine: A Problem in Historical Periodization', *Bulletin of the History of Medicine,* vol. 25, pp. 149-58.

Rosen, George (1963), 'Social attitudes to Irrationality and Madness in seventeenth and eighteenth century Europe', *Medical History,* vol. 18, pp. 220-40.

Rosen, George (1967a), 'People, Disease and Emotion: some newer problems for research in Medical history', *Bulletin of the History of Medicine,* vol. 41, pp. 5-23.

Rosen, George (1967b), 'Emotion and Sensibility in Ages of Anxiety: A Comparative Historical Review', *American Journal of Psychiatry,* 124, 6, pp. 771-84.

Rosen, George (1968a), 'Enthusiasm', *Bulletin of the History of Medicine,* vol. 42, no. 5, pp. 393-421.

Rosen, George (1968b), *Madness in Society,* London, Routledge & Kegan Paul.

Rosen, George (1975), 'Nostalgia: a "forgotten" psychological disorder', *Psychological Medicine,* vol. 4, no. 4, p. 340.

Rosenberg, Charles E. (1973), 'Sexuality, Class and Role in Nineteenth Century America', *American Quarterly,* vol. 25, no. 2, pp. 131-54.

Rosenthal, Leora N. (1977), 'The Definition of female sexuality and the status of women among Gujerati-speaking Indians of Johannesburg', in *The Anthropology of the Body,* ed. John Blacking, London. Academic Press.

Roth, Martin (1976), 'Schizophrenia and the Theories of Thomas Szasz', *British Journal of Psychiatry,* vol. 129, pp. 317-26.

Rothman, David (1971), *The Discovery of the Asylum,* Boston and Toronto, Little, Brown & Co.

Royal West of England Academy (1961), 'Bristol in the Evolution of Mental Health 1696-1961', *Exhibition Catalogue,* Bristol.

Scull, Andrew (1974), *Museums of Madness: the Social Organisation of Insanity in Nineteenth Century England,* Princeton University PhD.

Scull, Andrew T. (1975), 'From madness to mental illness: Medical men as moral entrepreneurs', *Archives Europeenes de Sociologia,* vol. 16, pp. 218-51.

Scull, Andrew T. (1977), *Decarceration: Community Treatment and the Deviant,* NJ, Prentice-Hall.

Scully, Diana and Bart, Pauline (1972-3), 'A Funny Thing Happened on the way to the orifice: Women in Gynecology Textbooks', *American Journal of Sociology,* vol. 78, no. 4, pp. 1045-50.

Sedgwick, Peter (1972), 'Mental Illness is Illness', *Salmagundi,* 20, pp. 196-225.

Shearyn, Phoebe (1909), *The Literary Profession in the Elizabethan Age,* 2nd edn. revised by J. W. Saunders, 1967, Manchester University Press.

Showalter, E. and Showalter, E. (1973), 'Victorian Women and Menstruation' in *Suffer and be Still,* ed. M. Vicinus, Bloomington and London, Indiana University Press, pp. 38-44.

Skae, David (1863), 'A Rational and Practical Classification of Insanity', *Journal of Mental Science,* 9, pp. 309-19.

Skultans, Vieda (1975), *Madness and Morals. Ideas on Insanity in the Nineteenth Century,* London, Routledge & Kegan Paul.

Smith—Rosenberg, Carroll and Rosenberg, Charles (1973), 'The Female Animal: Medical and Biological Views of Women and her Role in Nineteenth Century America', *Journal of American History,* vol. 60, pp. 332-56.

Smollett, Tobias (1960), *Humphrey Clinker.* New York Classics.

Spitzka, E. C. (1887), 'Cases of Masturbation', *Journal of Nervous and Mental Diseases,* pp. 238-9.

Street, Brian (1975), *The Savage in English Literature,* London, Routledge & Kegan Paul.

Stukeley, William (1723), *Of the Spleen.*

Swift, Jonathan (1939), *Prose Works,* ed. Herbert Davis, Oxford University Press.

Swift, Jonathan (1967), *Poetical Works,* ed. Herbert Davis, Oxford University Press.

Sydenham, Thomas (1848), *The Complete Works of Thomas Sydenham,* trans. from Latin ed. by R. G. Latham, London.

Szasz, Thomas (1971), *The Manufacture of Madness*, London, Routledge & Kegan Paul, Paladin, 1973.
Szasz, Thomas (1974), *Law, Liberty and Psychiatry: An Inquiry into the Social Uses of Mental Health Practices*, London, Routledge & Kegan Paul.
Szasz, Thomas (1976), 'The Sacred Symbol of Psychiatry', *British Journal of Psychiatry*, vol. 129, pp. 317-26.
Thackeray, William Makepeace (1887), *The Book of Snobs: Sketches of Life and Character*, London, Smith, Elder & Co.
Thomas, Keith V. (1958), 'Women and the Civil War Sects', *Past and Present*, no. 13.
Thomas, Keith V. (1959), 'The Double Standard', *Journal of the History of Ideas*, vol. 20, no. 2, pp. 195-216.
Thompson, Roger (1974), *Women in Stuart England and America*, London, Routledge & Kegan Paul.
Tibble, J. W. and Tibble, A. (1932), *John Clare: A Life*, London, Cobden-Sanderson.
Tourney, Garfield (1967), 'A History of Therapeutic Fashions in Psychiatry 1800-1966', *American Journal of Psychiatry*, 124, 6.
Tryon, Thomas (1683), *Healths Grand Preservative: or the Women's best Doctor*, London.
Tuke, Samuel (1813), *A Description of the Retreat – an Institution near York for Insane Persons of the Society of Friends*, revised edn. 1964, London, Dawsons.
Veith, Ilze (1956), 'On Hysterical and Hypochondrical Afflictions', *Bulletin of the History of Medicine*, vol. 30, pp. 233-40.
Viets, Henry R. (1949), 'George Cheyne 1673-1743', *Bulletin of the Institute of the History of Medicine*, vol. 23, Johns Hopkins University, pp.435-52.
Wain, John (1974), *Samuel Johnson*, London, Macmillan.
Walkington, Thomas (1607), *Optick Glasse of Humors on the Touchstone of a Golden Temperature, or the Philosophers Stone to Make a Golden Temple*.
Wallas, Ada (1929), *Before the Bluestockings*, London, Allen & Unwin.
Ward, Edward (1703), *The London Spy*, ed. Arthur L. Hayward, 1927, London, Cassell.
Ward, Edward (1704), *Female Policy Detected: or the Arts of a Designing Woman Laid Open*, London, B. Harris.
Watkins, W. B. C. (1960), *Perilous Balance. The Tragic Genius of Swift, Johnson and Sterne*, Cambridge.
Watt, Ian (1957), *The Rise of the Novel: Studies in Defoe, Richardson and Fielding*, Berkeley, University of California Press, pp. 140-146.
Webb, Sidney and Webb, Beatrice (1910), *English Poor Law Policy*, London, Longmans Green & Co.
Wesley, John (1747), *Primitive Physick*, revised edn. by A. W. Hill, London, Epworth Press.
Williamson, George (1935), 'Mutability, Decay and Seventeenth Century Melancholy', *Journal of English Literary History*, vol. 2, no. 3, pp. 121-50.

Willis, Thomas (1664), *The Anatomy of the Brain and Nerves,* McGill University Press, 1965.

Wilson, T. G. (1964), 'Swift and the Doctors', *Medical History,* vol. 8, pp. 199-216.

Wing, J. K. (1978), *Reasoning about Madness,* Oxford University Press.

Wood, Ann Douglas (1973), 'The fashionable diseases: women's complaints and their treatment in nineteenth century America', *Journal of Interdisciplinary History,* 4, 1973-4, pp. 25-52.

Woods, Evelyn A. and Carlson, Eric T. (1961), 'The Psychiatry of Philippe Pinel', *Bulletin of the History of Medicine,* vol. 35, pp. 14-25.

Woodward, John (1974), *To Do the Sick No Harm,* London, Routledge & Kegan Paul.

Woodward, John and Richards, David (eds.) (1977), *Health Care and Popular Medicine in Nineteenth Century England,* London, Croom Helm.

Wright, Louise B. (1935), *Middle Class Culture in Elizabethan England,* University of North Carolina Press, esp. Ch. 13, 'The Popular Controversy over Woman', pp. 465-507.

Wright, Thomas (1604), *The Passions of the Minde in Generall.* A reprint based on the 1604 edition with an Introduction by Thomas O. Sloan, Chicago, University of Illinois Press, 1971.

Zeldin, Theodore (1973), *France 1848-1945 Ambition, Love and Politics,* Oxford University Press.

Index

Cheyne's The English Malady

Burton's Anatomy of Melancholy — Humors / Milton

David Hartley's On Human Nature

Sympathy, Passion, Enthusiasm, Imagination, Reason

Mesmerism

Buchanad ? — & the Bible

Hysteria

Shift from religious authority

Phrenology

Byron & Tasso